TITANIA'S
NUMBER

TITANIA'S NUMBER

4

Titania Hardie

CONNECTIONS
BOOK PUBLISHING

For my reliable trio of 4s, Ian, Tessa and Robert, with love

A CONNECTIONS EDITION
This edition published in Great Britain in 2007 by
Connections Book Publishing Limited
St Chad's House, 148 King's Cross Road, London WC1X 9DH
www.connections-publishing.com

British Library Cataloguing-in-Publication data available on request.

ISBN 978-1-85906-226-5

1 3 5 7 9 10 8 6 4 2

Phototypeset in Bliss and Natural Script using QuarkXPress on Apple Macintosh
Printed in China

Contents

STARTING THE JOURNEY — 6

YOUR DAY NUMBER — 30

4'S CHARACTER — 32

4 AT WORK — 64

4'S CHILDHOOD — 85

4 AT PLAY — 108

4 IN LOVE — 118

4'S COMPATIBILITY — 131

4 IN OTHER PLACES — 210

YOUR LIFE NUMBER — 214

SAME DAY AND LIFE NUMBER — 217

DIFFERENT DAY AND LIFE NUMBERS — 223

THE FUTURE — 248

HOW TO FIND YOUR DAY AND LIFE NUMBERS — 270

FURTHER READING • ABOUT THE AUTHOR — 271

ACKNOWLEDGEMENTS — 272

STARTING THE JOURNEY

This little book of numerology invites you to be amazed by what you will learn from numbers – about your character, your tastes, your instincts, your relationships, and even about your future. But to do this involves a willingness to believe – as Pythagoras, the 'Father of Numbers' did – that numbers can provide a clue, or formula, through which we can perceive some of the evolving patterns and cycles that affect our own individual existence.

Let's find out more ...

Discovering numerology

Fans of Sudoku will understand how it entices us intellectually to see how strands of numbers — almost magically — slot together and interconnect with one another, revealing a rhythm of harmonious relationships between the lines. In one sense, numerology does this for us on a personal and spiritual level. The Science of Numbers, as it is called, suggests that there is an order and a rhythm in the universe of which we are a part, and although there is a certain mystery in the way numbers seem to function as symbols for our experiences, there is a long tradition across many cultures of their fascination for us.

Now, in an age of gigabytes, PINs and mathematic-based technology, how can we doubt the role that numbers play, or the way in which they have become part of our daily landscape? Numbers speak to us every day about our personal identity on this planet. Our birth date is absorbed by society as proof of our existence: you need it to be 'real' at the bank, in the office, when you travel, in an automated phone queue – in *all* official records. Indeed, many people consider the day-date of their birth-day to be their lucky number. But can it really say anything about us?

Did you know, for instance, that:

- If you were a **5** or a **9**, you'd need to invest in good-quality luggage because you'd be bound to notch up a lot of air miles?
- Or that a **6** feels compelled to generously host open-house for guests and family?
- A **7** will want to specialize in whatever interests them?
- And an **8** would rather have one small quality gift than half a dozen less luxurious presents?
- Or that a **3** is a born entertainer, who enjoys sharing time

4 5 6 7 8 9 1 2 3

with others, whereas a **2** prefers to live quietly, with just one or two partnerships, both socially and in business?

But you've picked *this* little volume because you're a **4**, numerology's most reliable number, and you will painstakingly spend hours getting something just right ... whereas if you were a **1**, you'd rush in and get several projects started, full of enthusiasm, only to leave someone else to carry them through to completion.

About this book

Each individual title in this series investigates, in depth, the meaning of one of nine personal numbers. *This* volume is dedicated to the exploration of the number **4**.

We will be focusing principally on your **DAY** number — that is, the number relating to the day of the month on which you were born (in your case, the 4th, 13th, 22nd or

31st of the month). Calculating your **DAY** number is easy: you simply add the digits of your day together (where applicable), and keep adding them until they reduce to a single number (*see calculation examples on page 270*). And that's it. It doesn't matter which month or year you were born in – you just need the day-date to discover your **DAY** number. And *you're* a **4**. (If you were born on the 22nd, this also gives you a 'master' number of **22**; we'll have something special to say about this later.)

Your **DAY** number reveals all kinds of information, and, working from this number, we will be considering:

- The obvious attributes of your number as they impact on your personality
- How you are likely to dress, and what colours or styles appeal
- How you react to things psychologically, and what drives or motivates you

4   5   6   7   8   9   1   2   3

- In which fields you will have the most natural abilities and gifts
- What annoys you most
- What sort of lover you are, and how you relate to all other numbers
- What the future holds

... and much, much more.

And you have another significant number too: your LIFE number. This is derived from adding up the digits in the *whole* of your birth date — day, month and year (*see examples on page 270*). What does *this* number mean, and what do your DAY and LIFE numbers mean in tandem? And how does it affect you if you're also a 'master' number (**11** or **22**)? Read on and you'll see. But first, let's meet your DAY number ...

3 2 1 9 8 7 6 5 4

So, you're a 4

Hard-working and thorough to a point of near-obsession at times, this is the number of careful plans and quiet application. **Steady** as a rock and unrelenting in adversity, **4** is the number of foundations well laid, like the symbol of a square, and it also encompasses the symbol of the family unit. Greater even than **2** at checking details, **4** is **methodical**, serious and conservative, but can sometimes lack a free imagination, or be too **cautious** to let a good imagination have free rein.

The projects around your home will be properly thought out, planned for and finished. Life is usually very **orderly**: papers filed, surfaces cleaned, cupboards neat and well-stocked. A **4**'s handbag or glove box probably contains the essentials for any emergency. But all the matters

4   5   6   7   8   9   1   2   3

you concern yourself with progress **slowly and carefully**, instead of great changes sweeping through on a regular basis. There is no point hurrying a **4**; life has its own rhythm around you.

According to the numbers in Genesis, the earth was made on the fourth day of the Creation. Symbolically, this suggests all that belongs to the earth is ruled by the number **4**. With this spirit as your daily inspiration you may love **growing** things – literally, getting your hands dirty – and you will **draw strength from nature**. If you are young and have not yet found the pleasure of a garden, it will almost certainly come to you.

This love of making things grow can also be seen in a metaphoric sense: you may love to **build** and shape physical structures, and you may be very adept with your hands. Many **4**s love DIY and handicrafts, and, if you work alongside a designer, **4** is the number to **actualize** many creative ideas, because no one has more skill and **tenacity** at achieving difficult projects than you. While others give up as soon as a plan hits a snag, you get into your stride and find a way through it, sometimes in a quite ferocious way. You are not aggressive, but you are **stubborn** and **determined** about finding a solution to a difficult task. **4** may not be a trailblazer, like **1**, but it is the steady tractor pushing over tough terrain and **getting the job done**. **4**s are the builders and the gardeners of the world.

Everyone comes to **rely on** number **4**, even if the methodical demands you make are sometimes a frustration for other numbers. Your **stability** is genuine: you can be counted on in a crisis. You recognize the importance of making a good **foundation** and building on it. There is a **no-nonsense** element in this, and public relations is something you can hardly be bothered with. Moreover, you are fully prepared to waive polite conversation to jump straight in and say exactly what you think. It is not so much tactlessness as **absolute honesty** that is the driving force behind this urge, but at times you do take friends and loved ones by surprise with your **frankness**. 4 is really a cautious number, taking things carefully and forming opinions slowly, but you will be very upfront once you have a clear view as you see it.

Traditions are important for you: you are aware of, and interested in, the way things have been done in the past. You may also have a high regard for established systems, and give a lot of your leisure time to historical and political interests. Somehow upholding the patterns of the past reinforces a sense of **security** in the here-and-now: you learn from previous mistakes and look to examples from your childhood and early life to avoid pitfalls in the future. This is all down to your **patience**, for no one is more patient than a person with a number **4** birthday.

If you have the letters 'D', 'M' or 'V' in your name (each of which has a value of **4** – more about this shortly), this would ensure that you use your innate feeling for order *constructively*; without these letters, you may feel you can never get things running sufficiently smoothly, and you may also be criticized for **extreme seriousness** and **lack of flexibility**, or your family life may be a little unstable or stressed. But your true colours – green, blue, and indigo – will bring you luck, as they are in harmony with **4's** strengths. You are related in many ways to the astrological earth sign Taurus – stubborn, but **reliable**.

Sound familiar? Getting a taste for what your number is about? And this is just the beginning. You'll soon find out how the number 4 expresses itself as your Day number in each and every day of your life. But before we go any further, let's take a look at where all this first came from . . .

4   5   6   7   8   9   1   2   3

What's in a number?

Numbers have always had a sacred meaning. The Egyptians used an alphabet that conflated letters and numbers, and, as such, each number exuded an idea that was more than the sum it stood for. There is a whole book of the Old Testament devoted to the subject; and the Hebrew language – exactly like the Egyptian – has a magical subtext of meaning where letters and numbers can be doubled to reveal an extra layer of secret, so-called 'occult' information. It is called the *gematria*, and forms a crucial part of the sacred occult wisdom called Kabbalah. There were twenty-two letters – a master number – in both the Greek (Phoenician) and Hebrew alphabets, and repetitions of the spiritual properties of the numbers **3** and, especially, **7** recur throughout the Bible.

3 2 1 9 8 7 6 5 4

The Father of Numbers

But modern numerology derives more formally from Pythagoras, the Father of Numbers, who was a serious and spiritual philosopher, as well as the man who explained some of the secrets of geometry. Born on the island of Samos, although he ultimately settled in Cretona, a Greek colony in southern Italy, he is understood to have travelled widely to both Egypt and Judea. Some accounts of his life also suggest he may have studied under the Persian sages of Zoroaster, but an analysis of his teachings certainly reveals the strong influence of Kabbalistic thought in his philosophy.

Pythagoras understood numbers as a *quality* of being, as well as a *quantity* of material value. In one sense, the numbers as figures were connected with the measuring of things, but 'number' itself was significantly different to this, and encompassed a spiritual value. The numbers from one through to nine represented universal principles through which everything evolves, symbolizing even the stages an idea passes through before it becomes a reality. Mathematics was the tool through which we could apprehend the Creation, the universe, and ourselves. Musical harmony was a sacred part of this knowledge, as was geometry, which revealed divine proportion.

Most importantly, Pythagoras believed that numbers were expressive of the principles of all real existence – that numbers themselves embodied the principles of our dawning awareness, our conjecture and growth. Through mathematics and number we could approach divine wisdom and the workings of the universe as a macrocosm. Thus, in microcosm, our personal 'mathematics' would unlock the workings of our own being, and help us to see a divine wisdom concerning ourselves. **1** was not just the first digit, but also had a character of beginning, of independence, of leadership, just as the number **2** was more than merely the second number quantifying two objects, but also implied the philosophical concept of a pair, of co-operation, of a relationship beyond the individual.

Pythagoras also believed that we could understand our direction and fate through an awareness of repeating cycles of number, making numerology a key to revealing our opportunities and our destiny.

By tradition, the doctrine Pythagoras taught to his students in the sixth century BCE was secret, and no one wrote down his ideas until his death. But Plato was a follower of Pythagoras and, along with the rebirth of Platonism, the ideas of the Father of Mathematics were revealed afresh during the revival of Greek learning in the Renaissance. The great magi of the fifteenth and sixteenth centuries explored anew the significance of number and the gematria, to understand the hidden messages of the ancients and of the divine mind. Mathematics as a philosophy was the bridge to higher realms of spirituality.

Essence of the numbers

one is the spark, the beginning, Alpha, the Ego of consciousness. It is male.

two is consort. Adding partnership, receptivity, it is female, bringing tact.

three is a synthesizing of both of these qualities and brings expansion and joy.

four is the number of the Earth, of the garden, and of stability. It brings order.

five is curiosity and experiment, freedom, changes. It brings sensuality.

six nurtures and cares for others. It will love and beautify, and brings counsel.

seven perfects and contemplates the Creation. It is intellect, stillness, spirit.

eight is the number of power, the octave, a higher incarnation. It brings judgement.

nine is humanity, selflessness, often impersonal and all-knowing. It brings compassion.

3 2 1 9 8 7 6 5 4

Applying the knowledge

A deeper understanding of the self can be achieved through an awareness of the mysticism of number within us; and both the birth date and, to some degree, our given name are the keys to unlocking our mystical, spiritual core of being. Exploring the affinity between letter and number can also reveal insights about the lessons we need to learn throughout our lives to improve and develop as individuals (*see page 25*).

This book looks at the significance of numbers as they affect us every day, focusing largely, as introduced earlier, on our **DAY** number. It is this number that reveals to us our instincts, our impulses, our natural tastes and undiluted responses, our talents and immediate inclinations. This is how people see us in daily situations, and how we behave by essence.

We will be exploring how our **DAY** number influences

4   5   6   7   8   9   1   2   3

our love relationships and friendships; at what it says about our career strengths and our childhood; at the way our number manifests in our leisure time; and at how it might give us a better understanding of what to expect in our future cycles, as we pass through any given year under the sway of a particular number. Each birthday initiates a new cycle, and each cycle seems uncannily connected with the philosophical concerns of the number which governs that year. Look both to the past and present to see how strongly the number-cycle can illuminate our experiences ... and then count ahead to ponder what may be in store over the next year or two.

And numbers also say something about where we live or work, about our car, and even about our pets. Understanding these secret qualities can add a new dimension of pleasure — not to mention surprise — to our journey through life.

3 2 1 9 8 7 6 5 4

A NUMBER TO GROW INTO

The presence of our **LIFE** number, however, takes longer for us to appreciate in ourselves – longer for us to grow into – and it often takes time to reveal itself. This number comes to the fore as your life progresses, and on pages 214–247 we will be looking at the meaning of your **DAY** number together with your individual **LIFE** number, to see what this reveals about your character and potentiality.

The **LIFE** number may intensify the experience of the **DAY** number – if it is closely related to it, or shares similar patterns. But more frequently our two different numbers clash a little, and this often allows insight into the aspects of our being where instinct pulls us in one direction but higher wisdom or experience mediates and pulls us in a second direction.

Who would have thought you could learn so much from a number? Pythagoras certainly did, over 2,500 years ago ... and now you will discover it too.

4   5   6   7   8   9   1   2   3

What's in a name?

Your name also has a story to tell, and it is a story revealed through number. Every letter corresponds to a number: in the Western alphabet we use twenty-six letters, which are at variance with the twenty-two formerly enshrined in the Hebrew and Greek alphabets. Some numerologists believe that this is in keeping with the more material world we now live in, as the number '26' reduces to '8' (when you add the digits), which is the number of power and money.

The correspondences between the numbers and the letters of the alphabet are as follows:

1	2	3	4	5	6	7	8	9
A	B	C	D	E	F	G	H	I
J	K	L	M	N	O	P	Q	R
S	T	U	V	W	X	Y	Z	

3	2	1	9	8	7	6	5	4

As you are a **4**, it is most revealing to look at the letters D, M and V as they occur (or not!) in your name. This is because they intensify the experience and impression of your main number.

To make the most of the qualities inherent in your number, you should be using a name which is in poetic harmony with your DAY number. As a **4**, you will exude sense and logic at its best if you have a name which underlines these **4** qualities. Using a name which includes a D, M or V bolsters your powers. If this sounds strange, consider that many of us have our names shortened or played upon by friends, family and lovers, so it is important to feel that our chosen name – the one that we use as we go about in the world – is making the best of our abilities and energies.

Among the letters that are equivalent to the number **4**, D and M are common consonants, so the chances are that you have one of these letters in your name. It is especially significant if your name starts with one of these letters, for it introduces the strength of your number **4** right at the beginning of your name. Create a nickname with these letters in, if necessary, just to back up the outstanding properties of creativity that come with your number.

The letter-numbers help us to act out our sense of purpose, and if these work in correspondence with the **DAY** number we are more likely to find our sense of will and achieve our goals more rapidly. But if we have few, or none, of the letters of our **DAY** number, we often feel it is much harder to shine in our field of opportunity.

Missing a '4' letter?

As a **4**, you rely on method and practicality to negotiate daily challenges, but without a '**4**' letter in your name you'll need to work on finding a way to harness your time efficiently. You may also find your natural sense of diligence is constantly tested, if you are lacking an active '**4**' letter.

3	2	1	9	8	7	6	5	4

Those without a single '**4**' letter will find it difficult to budget and knuckle down to duty – something that is crucial if you are a **4**. They may also be particularly brutal in their honesty – too much so – and end up hurting others unintentionally. Find a way to include one of the letters you lack. This is also important with regard to your physical health, which is so necessary to your sense of identity. Without a '**4**' letter you will struggle to feel physically ready to take on the duties before you. It is important that you boost your sense of self in any way you can to offset this, as you feel (possibly rightly) that people are relying on your physical and mental stamina. If you are choosing a business name, then, you must bear this in mind.

Too many 'D's or 'M's?

It can be just as much of a problem if your name carries a flood of letters which correspond to your number. This potentially gives you an overdose, and brings out some of the more negative qualities associated with **4**. Too many '**4**' letters may make you too tied to home and security. If you have three or more 'D's and three or more 'M's, you may be too stubborn and totally inflexible, a person who cannot bear change so much so that any alterations make you bad-tempered and unreasonable. Emotional break-downs may come through overwork and a tendency to hide behind your obligations. You may feel you carry too many burdens and have little support from others.

If V is a prominent letter in your name, you have the 'master' letter matching number **22**. You are an excellent worker, and either very practical or totally impractical! The letter – just like the master number – has a duality in its nature. Which are you?

3 2 1 9 8 7 6 5 4

YOUR DAY NUMBER
It's a new day ...

You will learn a lot about the numbers of your birthday and your name as this book unfolds, but the DAY number is, to my mind, the most important – and sometimes least well-recognized – number of all ... the number which exerts a magnetic hold on us each and every day of our lives. Every time we react to a situation, an emotion, a provocation of any kind, we are shooting straight from the hip, as it were, and this reaction is coloured by our DAY number.

As we know, your 'Day Force', or DAY, number is **4** if you were born on the 4th, 13th, 22nd or 31st of any month. Each of these different dates also affects us – the charac-

| 4 | 5 | 6 | 7 | 8 | 9 | 1 | 2 | 3 |

teristics of the number derived from a birthday on the 13th vary intriguingly from one on the 22nd, for instance (especially given the added master-number dimension) — and we will look at these differences in the pages ahead.

All four dates, however, still reconcile to an overall **4**. This number determines your gut reactions and the way you express yourself when you are being most true to yourself. Your parents, lovers, friends and co-workers all know you best through this number.

So what is the theme of being a 4? What are you like when you're at work, rest and play? And how compatible are you with the other numbers? Let's find out ...

| 3 | 2 | 1 | 9 | 8 | 7 | 6 | 5 | 4 |

4'S CHARACTER
Charms, graces, warts and all ...

The one person who can see the possibility of turning dreams into reality, 4s are not known for their creativity or imagination, and yet this number is a great builder and can transform thought into fact. With the ability to sort the wheat from the chaff, you are acutely aware of what is of material value, and where to place your energies to distil that value. Often using mathematical thinking as an underpinning, your mental energies are sound and consistent, and you have exactly what it takes to see an arduous task or extensive project all the way to its conclusion – no matter how much focus that demands.

Blessed with extraordinary stamina and physical courage, little anyone else can say will dissuade you from a course of action once you have decided upon it: and if that means going it alone at times, you can manage. Dependent on no one more than yourself, **4**s are fearless about the demands of a rocky landscape or a hot climate, when either are to be negotiated to achieve a goal.

You can count on me

You often get unfair press for being too sensible and hard-working. Some may think of you as the embodiment of the saying 'all work and no play' makes for a dull boy, but this is not an even assessment. Though a very negative **4** may show signs of extreme seriousness, or an unhealthy obsession with facts and detail at the expense of a more accurate complete picture, the majority of **4**s constitute the most dependable of all numbers, with extraordinary powers of concentration and a skill for finding the method with which to attack – and attain – the greatest heights.

You're the keyholder to some of the ideas and creative urges of other numbers, and you know better than most how to break down a seemingly impossible task and turn it into something achievable. This is because of your pragmatism, and your ability to see through the excitement that gets a plan off the ground: you know how to follow that initial but short-lived burst of enthusiasm with real application and the method needed to build the idea into a reality. If a **1** or **5** is the architect, a **4** is the master builder working with masons to grind through the hidden demands of a big venture. Almost certainly you are logical, and clever with your hands. **4**s are the workers of the planet – the cornerstone for making ideas of progress into solid truths. And you can go it alone when others tire, too!

Without necessarily being reasonable in everything (for **4** gets its little likes and dislikes, which no one can soften!),

Keynotes of the 4 personality

Positive associations: integrity, high moral values, serious mind, even temperament, courage, patience, perseverance, good grasp of facts, hard-working, logical, appreciation for law and legal matters

Negative associations: unimaginative, overly serious, relatively fixed opinions, inability to cope with change, can be argumentative if challenged, too exacting and conservative

yours is nearly always a rational number, and yet it also has quite a spiritual dimension. Philosophical musings, though, must be sensible ideas, easy to grasp and to explain, for them to appeal to you. With a respect for thoughts and cultural beliefs which have gone before, you like to understand what is *behind* a spiritual idea; then, you will have much to contribute about it, and with sound discussion.

3   2   1   9   8   7   6   5   4

You will refuse to believe in myth outright, but may have an interest in the truths that were absorbed in its creation, often looking for the fire beneath the smoke. In a similar way, your artistic merits are built on solid blocks: many **4**s are very musical, which may arise out of a facility with maths, and you probably have the patience to train untiringly at any chosen skill, knowing that hard graft is always behind success, even when it appears to be attained effortlessly. **4**s frequently achieve a destiny in music, or even stage and theatre, because of their groundedness, while other more flamboyant and overtly arty people have no follow-through, and can only dream of their goal.

Salt of the earth

As **4** is so strongly connected with the laws of the earth, you are probably green-fingered and love your garden. You may see reason in spending time and energy in nurturing plants and vegetables when everything else seems to be in chaos. Like Voltaire's Candide, you'll see the sense in digging in the garden to build something when all else is failing. Even if you only have a small patio, you're usually delighted to get your hands dirty and grow something. Given space, yours will be the best vegetable or herb garden, because these plants have both an aesthetic and a practical function; you like things that are real, that you can hold onto. And you have the perseverance to bring tiny little seedlings into healthy little plants – metaphorically speaking, too.

It matters very little that you are not usually the originator of ideas (unless your LIFE number is a highly creative one; *see page 214*): you are the one to get anything done if it can be done – which makes you the best employee, or the hardest worker. Even if you work in a large organization, you need no one to oversee what you're doing, for you are perfectly self-reliant and happy to work without much thanks. You do always prefer order around you to function well, and an untidy room or desk, or sloppy co-workers, will impede you. You like to arrange a system that others are happy to copy, and you also have a reputation for honesty and straight-talking to others about what you are doing. You will say what you think, and be counted on for your common-sense appraisal. You may well encounter a constant stream of hard knocks and sharp falls, but you have the mettle to pick yourself up and go on. Your courage is applauded by everyone who knows you.

Preparation, preparation, preparation

You dislike people who are too gullible, and have a need to make certain that an idea or an expression is true and reliable. This makes you a good researcher and writer, though a **4** is better suited to writing non-fiction than fiction. If any career requires patience and care, the assembling of facts and details, the necessity of obtaining clearances and

4   5   6   7   8   9   1   2   3

permissions, **4** is the number for that job. You have such determination, coupled with a calm attitude, always aware of the subtext behind any project when others are surprised at what they have bitten off. You are always prepared, and your perseverance can be befuddling to others.

Yet you rarely take on a project or agree to a venture – even a social outing – unless it seems to have real worth. You are very good at assessing what has value, and many friends will look to you to decide just that – what has merit and what is a pipe dream. You'll make mistakes sometimes, sure, but are generally prepared to own up to them – and you never make the same mistake twice. Your natural sense of industry is married to the inclination to learn in the field. Experience teaches you, and you are willing to learn.

Try to be alive to the possibility that your opinions are sometimes just too fixed, and be willing to listen to other options before you settle on an important path. Difficulty may come from being too intent on detail, to the point where you are slow off the mark and miss an opportunity ... though sometimes this propensity will also turn out in your favour, and illustrate the moral of the hare and the tortoise. You usually get there in the end.

Getting results

Though always industrious and honest, this becomes especially so with the master-number variation of **4: 22**. If this is your number, you have a strong guiding sense that work must not be for selfish purposes, and that you have obligations to those in the world besides yourself. We'll take a look at this in greater detail shortly (*see page 56*), but what we can say here is that all **4**s like to contribute to a tangible result – to see and achieve something better than what was there before. This can mean that **4** gives too much to others – especially family – and that you may make a martyr of yourself to a career cause.

Anyone with the number **4** probably feels a push to be active rather than inactive, but often your working life may seem too dull and routine, precisely because others rely on you to wade through tedious and demanding chores – and know that you can do it. Eventually, you will rise to the top – and perhaps find other, younger, **4**s who are in the process of gaining the very experience that got you there, who will do the duties below you.

Questions, questions …

With a strong interest and good intelligence for natural laws and principles, you may have a good scientific mind, and understand complex ideas that leave others in the dark. Your grasp of logic is particular, and you can go at things thoroughly until you understand them fully. You may ask numerous questions until you're satisfied, and drive others mad, but won't rest until you've got to the inner workings

3   2   1   9   8   7   6   5   **4**

of a concept. This makes you a good delver, unafraid to dive in and stir up a hornet's nest to find out 'why' or 'how'. Others, perhaps, take this on faith, but you? Never!

You have strong opinions about what is ethical, and you are regarded by some as old-fashioned in your sense of right and wrong, especially with regard to relationships. Sometimes this means you place a lot of expectation on those you love, asking them to live up to your high standards. Equally, you would rather move within the rules than break them – which may be wise, but you can be the last to seize new ways of doing things, or to keep up-to-date with modern technology. What's important is that you try to let those you work and live with find their own way and experiment more than you may want to. You like to live within secure parameters, but others may want to take risks, and it can be traumatic for you watching someone you love taking chances. This is a battle you are likely to be faced with regularly – and it never seems to get any easier!

Teach us a lesson

As stalwart workers with an enviable selflessness, 4s are often the educators of the world. Teaching appeals to you, and you give a great deal if you are called on to lecture or teach. Able to sustain concentration for long periods, you find it easy to accept all the concomitant duties of teaching, and the research, marking and preparation of lessons is par for the course. This makes you very good at the bureaucratic side of teaching work, too, and many 4s find a niche working in the business side of creative fields, such as publishing or media.

And, even if 4s are not creating the ideas, they may be evolving them and delivering the necessities to make them happen. You may also want to further your *own* education gently throughout your life: 4 never knows enough to satisfy its thirst for sound knowledge, so be prepared to feel like a lifelong student, one way or another.

3 2 1 9 8 7 6 5 4

A little more flexibility?

The negative side of your number, which has been touched on already, is at its worst when you are either too slow in your assessments and actions or too fastidious. It is not always possible to have ideal conditions for work or relationships, and you may have to be more flexible in this regard. It is also a factor for **4** that the number goes with moodiness, and often the inevitable placing of too many burdens on your strong shoulders leads you to feel resentful and grumpy. Try not to let this resentment build up, and work to find a way to accept that others think differently to you, or have expectations of their own.

If you can't find a way to come to terms with this, and resign your determination to convert others to your viewpoint at all costs, you may become dissatisfied and sterile in your view of the world. You may even become too trapped in your own world, and find that you're alone. But

4   5   6   7   8   9   1   2   3

a positive **4** will always see reason in the end, and this – coupled with hard work and perseverance in all things – is usually your real strength and salvation.

4 in a nutshell

Personality watchwords: constructive outlook, urge to make a useful world, dependable

Lucky colours: blue, green, indigo

Lucky herbs/flowers: courgette flower, mint, borage, clover, pansy

Scents: bergamot, lime, pine, ginger

Fashion style: tailored, neat, conservative but high quality

Decorative style: clean space, good light, love of antiques, prefers old houses

Letters: D, M or V (needed in the name you use)

Car style: Four-by-four! Solid and thoroughly dependable

Holiday destination: classical locations, countryside (where 4 would prefer to live!)

Which 4 are you?

9 1 2 3 **4** 5 6 7 8

Everyone with a **DAY** number of **4** will exhibit many of the characteristics just discussed. It is interesting to see, though, how the number **4** varies across all of its incarnations. There is a subtle but definite difference between the way the number operates for someone born on the 4th of the month – which makes for a pure **4** effect – and someone born, say, on the 22nd (a master number).

As a rule, anyone born on the single-digit date has the truest and most undiluted effect from the number, whereas someone born as a product of two digits borrows some qualities from the pairing of the numbers. Twenty-anything puts the softening digit '2' before the second

4 5 6 7 8 9 9 1 2 3

number, and this usually means that, whatever number you are, you are more aware of the needs of others. Similarly, if '1' is the first digit (13th), you are more independent, and perhaps more assured of your self-worth, than **4** people are generally. And the '3', in 31st, adds an extra dimension from the number **3** itself — you have borrowed something from **3**'s charisma and charm!

Let's look at the variations across all the birthdays ...

3   2   1   9   8   7   6   5   4

Born on the 4th?

A birthday on the 4th suggests you are a hard-working and apparently well-organized person with a strong natural ability in all kinds of business. Your career, in fact, will be part of your whole life to you, not just part of a working day. Whatever you choose to do work-wise is a statement of the person you are. You can be the most economical and conscientious of the **4** variations, and a job left to you for completion will always be in excellent hands – no matter how banal and irksome it may seem to others. You are practical, and lay solid foundations to build up your world. Your honesty and forthrightness ensure your success in all you do, and you are probably deeply respected.

Loyalty is one of your most powerful characteristics, and you also love rules and regulations in your life. You gain admiration from loved ones and, especially, from co-

4   5   6   7   8   9   1   2   3

workers, for these attributes manifest every single day of your life, in a dozen ways; everyone knows you as wise and fair. You do also have a very emotional nature, though, and, in spite of your apparent caution about life, your feelings – once given – run very deep. However, you may be disinclined to show this, due to your practical and careful nature, and subsequently perhaps receive few of the overt tokens of love that you really deserve just as much as other people do. Never let it be said that you are unromantic – but you may have to learn to unleash this part of yourself, so that others come to realize it too, and you should certainly find a way to express your emotions to the person who counts most to you.

You are an indefatigable worker when inspired, and you will be able to drive others – as well as yourself – to finish a job within the deadline. What you must guard against is the possibility of driving yourself too hard and allowing your health to suffer as a consequence. It will help if you burn one of your signature oils (*see 'scents' on page 47*) – especially the bergamot – to combat stress and exhaustion, which you are prone to.

4s are good workers at whatever they do, but you have a particular talent for creating or discovering practical gifts and items for the home; indeed, such an interest would make a good business for you. But because your birthday is the pure **4**, your natural inclination might also be towards building and architecture – and all things connected with it – as well as any work requiring careful concentration or use of the hands. Business, banking, clerical work, accounting, draughting and design, writing, managing, statistical work, hard-graft secretarial (a personal assistant whose job is largely to organize someone else, for instance), computing, or businesses connected with property/insurance, are obvious outlets for your skills. You may also simply have the urge to grow things – and **4** is always the number of the nurseryperson and landscape gardener.

| 4 | 5 | 6 | 7 | 8 | 9 | 1 | 2 | 3 |

Your most negative traits centre on stubbornness, and being far too set in your ways. Some might think you too blunt in the way you express yourself, but this stems from a basic need for directness. You dislike change, being on the conservative side, and you must try something out for yourself before you will give it credence. But your loyalty, once given to a person, place or thing, is given for always.

Born on the 13th?

People fear that the 13th is an unlucky birthday, but this is not really so. The number is often misunderstood and given all kinds of negative connotations because of its connection with Death in the tarot ('Death' is card XIII in the Major Arcana), but it is not concerned with death in the ordinary sense. It is, of course, the witches' number, for there are thirteen moons in a year, which witches work by, and this makes it a number of power, mystery and challenge.

What you should understand is that, if you are born on this day, you will work especially hard for the things that really matter to you. The number is concerned with the constant 'death' of circumstances – or, in other words, change – and this is not always palatable to a **4**. But you do have a stronger philosophical sense than most other variants of **4**, and this will help you to cope. You are also more strongly driven.

You have a superb prowess in managerial and detailed work, and you have a better understanding of other people's suffering than any other **4** birthday. You are entirely loyal and honest, accurate in work demanding great concentration, and you have a forceful ambition. You will succeed best if your home is stable and your family life strong and supportive – but this is just the thing that is often tested in the life of a young '13'. In fact, you need security very badly, and you may go to great lengths to experience this in the light of much pressure in your early life. You can be terribly tenacious about relationships, hard to shake off a particular course or affection when you have set your mind to it, no matter how hopeless it may seem. You can be dictatorial too, and relentlessly unforgiving if someone offends you really deeply.

You work hard and propel others to the same level of

performance, but you are also very sensitive, and may truly suffer if you feel oppressed by a limited environment. You are deeply loving and actually very sensuous – more so than other 4s – but are perhaps frightened to demonstrate this. You will get into difficulty as a result of being often misunderstood, even by those who believe they know you well. You can be temperamental, but you are also inspirational and powerful if your forcefulness is directed well. Remember that, as 13 is the witches' number, it bestows great psychic and intuitive gifts, and an excellent facility for seeing the whole picture, rather than just the minutiae which often tie down 4's impetus. Yours is the number of wisdom from experience: use your knowledge.

As far as your career goes, you belong squarely in the business world. Though not really a leader, you do pick up the challenge for others, and you have the basic organizational abilities common to all 4s. You would thrive in, and enjoy, accounting, building, property, architecture, merchandising, buying, and working with gems or minerals. With your sense of other people, you would be an excellent archaeologist or historian, because, like many **4**s, you have talent for writing. Your forte would be in report-making or journalism, which both require practical skills and research ability, as well as mental concentration.

As a '13', don't let the frequent tests of your courage and stamina drive you to pursue transient satisfactions. Drinking or eating too much, and difficult relationships, often plague this variation of **4** when the going gets tough. You can become very self-destructive when in a gloomy mood. But you have a talent for utilizing the very things others would discard, and when you use your psychic abilities – which are unusual in **4**s – you have the tools to see right through, and into, people and situations.

Born on the 22nd?

Like **11**, yours is a master number which always uses the power of both digits to operate. Sacred to the number of letters in the Greek and Hebrew alphabet, **22** is full of higher consciousness and possibility. This birthday belongs to the unusual – the seeker after life's special doctrines, the person who is determined to perfect any task and utilize any opportunity. Both inspired and practical, imaginative and conservative, **22** can be highly strung and live (some-how!) off its nervous energy. Almost absurdly hard-working and dedicated to whatever it has given its cause to, this number demands – and gets – a command performance from those who hold it as a birthday number.

With so many talents to choose from, it can be diffi-cult for a **22** to know which basket is the better to place most of its creative eggs – and yet the truth is that most

22s have a light within that directs them from an early age. Highly intelligent and somewhat impatient with others of less ability, you will almost certainly leave your home town to make a success of your life elsewhere. You may be a handful for your parents, ask too many questions, say things that seem to come from another space or viewpoint. You need to escape in order to realize your full and exceptional potential.

Your determination is persuasive to other people, and you can accomplish anything you desire. Master builder and master writer, you have an altruism and a vision for the whole of humanity which drives you to make the choices that you do. Yours is not the destiny of mortals – but this is not always an especially cosy or flattering idea. Relationships may suffer as a result of your incredible drive and dedication to a cause or career; not everyone who shares your life will be accommodating about this. You are a humanitarian, and your thinking is consequently global rather than parochial. But might your family feel neglected because of this?

You have immense charm and wit – though sometimes it can be cynical if you feel you are dealing with fools – and you have the talent and largesse to organize and inspire others without being high-handed. Your intuition is excellent and your first impressions about people are usually spot-on. All your talents give you the potential to attract wealth and prestige ... but this may not be what's important to you. A synthesizing power of rational thought helps you see the way to achieve truly enormous goals – perhaps as a politician, surgeon, writer, broadcaster or philanthropist. Musical, like other **4**s, you are the soloist or composer, able to articulate others' pain. And even when your opinions are fixed – again, a common **4** trait – you will have come to your viewpoint through personal suffering and deep contemplation. Your wisdom is held in awe by most people.

Is there nothing bad to say? Actually, you can be the most difficult child — perhaps too self-resourceful, with a very high IQ and a low boredom threshold. Or possibly you are never satisfied, and become an obsessive perfectionist. There is perhaps a fine line between genius and folly, but you are someone who will work hard to test the limit of our human potential. No problem is outside your reach of mental acuity, and you are destined eventually to find answers that elude others. As long as your ego doesn't get in the way, this should be a prompt to use your talents for the betterment of others. Likely, this is how you will use them. Just don't ask for a trouble-free ride in your personal life while you achieve all of this!

Born on the 31st?

This is the best **4** birthday for business and organization, and if you develop your practicality to a high degree you will be very successful in your life, in terms of both money and career accolades. Co-operation is necessary in your daily landscape, as is the need for careful direction of your relationships and affairs, but with your variation of the **4 DAY** number you will usually be long-lived and physically robust, a true achiever and a hard worker. You will always repay kindnesses, and have a long memory for people who have helped you. Try to keep your aspirations within reach, to avoid inescapable disappointments, but, most importantly, don't take on too much at one time.

You are very loyal to any cause you take to heart, and to family, colleagues and friends. Dominant and determined, you'll exert tremendous effort to achieve your desired end.

| 4 | 5 | 6 | 7 | 8 | 9 | 1 | 2 | 3 |

You enjoy travel, but love returning home, and shouldn't live alone, as your family and close friends form an important part of your support network. You are well suited to marriage or responsible relationships, and, borrowing from the nature of the number **3**, you really adore your children.

Having the same flair for accounting as all **4**s, but to a particularly highly developed degree, you can be very thrifty and honest, and will prefer keeping your financial affairs in good order. If your environment is well arranged, you will function more efficiently, but you will resent anyone's interference in your methods. You can be very, very stubborn about this, and it takes a particular individual to function smoothly with you at work or in the home. This is part of your appeal, though, as well as a difficulty – for you are very independent and quite proud, and you can be very determined to prove a point.

Health and its associated subjects will always be of interest. You may be acutely aware of diet and hygiene, and will have a logical understanding of drugs and herbals, cures and first-aid procedures. Indeed, many people with this birthday choose medicine as a career. You would also succeed very well in projects concerning building and property investments, and in all forms of contracting, accountancy, writing, clerical and book work, illustrating, and work with health foods. Quite naturally, you acquire knowledge though research and deeper self-education.

Your worst flaw is probably that you have a confused reaction to change, and an inclination to obsessive exactness. Friends may not always know how to cope with this, and your family may not feel they can live up to it. If you've had a particularly conventional upbringing, you may also be very serious indeed, and unable to laugh at yourself when things go awry. Don't let this prevent you from using your tremendous strength to start again if need be, and have the last laugh on those who doubted the wisdom of your path.

4   5   6   7   8   9   1   2   3

The other thing to be aware of is a tendency to decide for others, based on what seems to be their best interests. This is part of your protective and solid nature, but you must accept that others will make their own mistakes and discover what they may in their own time and way. Be as patient as possible, and remember that — despite your strong will and excellent, forceful determination — what is right for you may not be right for someone else.

Ambition comes to someone with this number — more than for most **4**s. This ambition may not be of a traditional kind (to achieve more than others); it may be that you are driven to do things better, or more inventively, than other people. This is because the number **1** rests in your birth date, so the power and physical stamina of **1** is present alongside the more important **4**. Perhaps, because of this, you love a good fight, and are determined to combat obstacles. But what an exhilaration you feel when you win through!

3 2 1 9 8 7 6 5 4

4 AT WORK

So, what kind of employee does your number make you? We've already seen that your birthday suggests you are much more comfortable working in a close partnership, but when you're in a group, how do you fit in? If you're the boss, are you a good one? Which fields are likely to be the best for your talents? And which the worst? And what about the male/female divide? Is a 4 female boss more desirable than a 4 male colleague?

Here, we get to grips with your career potential, your needs and 'must-have's for job satisfaction, and your loves and loathes work-wise, hopefully highlighting some areas where there is room for you to adjust your manner around others, to help you achieve what it is you're aiming for.

In the marketplace

Your number might be deemed the 'I can' of numerology, rather like the first Earth sign of the zodiac, Taurus. This means that, whether you are just starting out at work or are a seasoned professional, your spirit is always determined to find a way to succeed at any task you are set — like a rite of passage.

You are likely to make an impression very early on in any job, with your willingness to focus on a direction and tick it off the 'to do' list as quickly as possible — not that you rush through your work, though. You are thorough and careful, but you will click along and keep on something until it is in the 'out' tray. You are not someone whose attention craves constant variety, or who skips from one thing to another. You are enviably able to stay on track until a job is done.

3   2   1   9   8   7   6   5   4

STAYING POWER

You love responsibility, even if it means the buck stops with you. While many numbers enjoy the idea of getting something under way, you are made for the duties of following up, uncovering hidden data that is needed to progress, and having the staying power to get right through a project, from start to finish.

No other number has such steadfast determination. You need to see results, whatever your work, and you take great pride in a job well done. But here you have the advantage on other numbers, because the pride is in the work and the result achieved, rather than born out of any need to feed your ego and tell yourself that you have done something special. You are also able to see results coming together long before others realize that things are taking shape. You have the power to see right through, and to recognize that progress — however slow — is being made, which others cannot see.

Most people will probably tell you that they see you as a careful worker who doesn't like to take unnecessary chances, or get into risky situations. You are a good economist, and you impose a reassuring, natural authority over the financial aspects of a job – which others look to you to do. Well-organized accounts and nimble money-handling may excite you in a way that leaves others open-mouthed, which makes you the best person to assign to any work that includes contracts, budgets or scheduling of any kind. Making things run smoothly is a pleasure to you, and you can always find a better way of doing this than whoever preceded you in this role. Your unerring ability to evaluate a job in terms of its worth and potential yield makes other people's workloads lighter. And, simply because you have this capacity to analyse what is involved in a job, you can rise to the position of boss or chief without ever seeming ambitious.

WHERE DOES YOUR LIGHT REALLY SHINE?

Here are some of the qualities that **4**s bring to any job:

- A willingness always to muck in, no matter how odious a task may be, makes you an inspiration to others, who may consequently become somewhat less precious in their own demands. You give your team of co-workers perspective: nothing is beneath anyone when there's a job at stake.

- Your sense of method supports a mind that makes calm value judgements about the requirements of any project, which makes it a pleasure for others to have you on board. You often minimize the sense of panic around you, as you will find the way to get through almost anything.

- Honest and hard-working to the core, your CV will grow long with praise for your diligence and reliability. Many will tease you for this, but it is a base requirement in any job, and you leave others standing as you rise naturally through the ranks, thanks to your renowned dependability.

- Contrary to perception, you have an excellent character and suitability for creative work, being able with your hands and capable of detailed work, but also prepared for long (often thankless) grinding hours. You will be delighted to be a part of making or marketing anything, as long as it's useful: quality and utility are more significant for you than mere aesthetics.
- Where a **3** would flinch (or have a breakdown!) when forced into routine work, you enter the fray with a wry look and take on whatever they turn their nose up at. Seeing temperamental peers as prima donnas, you show them the way and quickly take control in a shaping crisis. The laugh is on them!

In short, building useful and tangible products or networks, being a rock for others to lean on, unearthing ways of

3   2   1   9   8   7   6   5   4

doing the difficult jobs, keeping your cool in a dirty or less-than-ideal environment ... These are the characteristics of a **4** at work. Without outward flamboyance, you find a way to minimize fuss and maximize efficiency, and, though you yourself might agree that it is for the **1**s and **5**s to generate ideas, you are the one who translates such plans from drawing board to reality. The result is that you are over-relied on! Fields which lend themselves to the expression of your talents include ...

Banking and finance Your management of money and the feeling of security you generate make you an ideal accountant or financial adviser. You have the right mind-set to approach such work with enthusiasm and self-respect. Moreover, your extraordinary personal stability – as others perceive you – sends out the right message, and you are very possibly headed for the manager's job.

| 4 | 5 | 6 | 7 | 8 | 9 | . | 1 | 2 | 3 |

Real estate/property development A deep desire to build and an appreciation for property makes this an excellent vocation for a **4**, as you also emit a persona of trustworthiness to your clients. Even if your business is in another field, property – as a hobby or as part of your personal landscape – is likely to prove a successful field for improving your own finances. You will speculate with intelligence, make sound investments and handle your moves deftly. Everything connected with the house is a potential area of financial success for you.

Law The legal field is an excellent arena for **4**. Whether you become an Ally McBeal-type, who can move juries through emotional truths, or a potential partner in a *Boston Legal* firm, battling the world on issues of moral integrity, you have just what it takes to project honesty and diligence without flashy fireworks. All kinds of corporate law and legal training regarding contracts should be looked after by **4**.

3   2   1   9   8   7   6   5   4

Religion Religious or spiritual expression is often part of **4**'s make-up, and it is not surprising to find your number working contentedly in such a vocation. The ministry, church charities, or more modern manifestations of religious thought often attract **4**s – partly because you have a strong sense of what is right and wrong. Religious philosophy can be a guide-rail for many, and this is where it belongs firmly within **4**'s world – giving shape and tradition when it is needed, and offering comfort to many.

Mathematics and science These are subjects a **4** can handle with skill, and any work which demands a knowledge of either will suit you. This embraces everything from teaching to nursing, which demands hard slog along with the scientific understanding of medicine and the human body, to surgery, which utilizes the manual dexterity for which **4**s are famed, to IT, which requires long hours of focused, careful, precise work. The geologist and the biochemist, the researcher and naturalist — all make demands that can be furnished from **4**'s portfolio of talents.

Business and retail work These fields are made for a **4**. Who else has the wherewithal to negotiate such a variety of differing tasks and skills, to assemble such a panoply of facts, to attend to so much detailed data, and keep smiling? Being strong, physically and mentally, you are the one who can sift through all the minutiae, doing the accounts and costing, assembling the personnel information, filling out forms and managing paperwork, ordering stock. You can also stand up for hours when you have to! When sheer slog is demanded, you are there.

Publishing You will always find a **4** in publishing. My own experience proves that editors, who must comb the text for mistakes and lapses of authorial sense, tend to be **4**s. The very characteristic of being systematic and, perhaps, a little unimaginative makes **4** so good at this job – and, again, in all the requirements of production and overseeing others' creativity, **4** is the ideal person. Not to do you a disservice, you have a great facility with writing, especially when common sense and clarity are required. Journalism is also an excellent path for you to follow, because of the need to dig out facts and gain others' trust, to get them to talk.

Farming/agriculture Work on the land, and with animals, also comes under the domain of a **4**. Farms, fields, gardens, food produce ... all belong to you; and when a vet is needed who can wade into the pig sty with her best shoes on in an emergency, **4** is never faint-hearted. And you can see the funny side of every disaster – usually!

This list isn't exhaustive – a **4** will find a way of bringing their strengths to any job – but it does offer a good idea of the kinds of subject that should appeal to your number. Whatever the field, the need to see something material take shape is at the root of **4**'s business talent.

And for luck?

Whatever your work, you will achieve your maximum potential if you use a name to work with that includes the letters D, M or V. Remember this when you are choosing a company name, if you go into partnership. It will help, too, for you to optimize your energy and positive attitude, if you decorate your work environment in the indigo/green colours of the sea. If you are going for an important interview, these colours would make a positive choice in your outfit, as they help you to project yourself in your secure and sensible light.

3 2 1 9 8 7 6 5 4

WORK PROFILE
The 4 female boss

Unruffled in heatwave conditions, and **single-mindedly** pursuing a point others have forgotten was significant, the **4** female boss is a model of business skill. Never resorting to the need for flattery or showy behaviour, she has earned her place by simply being the **best** and most **assured** member of a team, always **one step ahead** with a ready supply of data, and always aware that just one more step than others realize is required to achieve a contract. She **saves the day** time after time, with her **anticipation** for what will be involved in any work plan. Quite probably cool and collected in couture – for **4** women realize that money spent on designer clothes brings a lasting return – the **4** female boss can answer any sudden demand on her attention, and return with **precision** to where she left off when the knock came at her door.

Hardly power-crazy, she is just as **ready** to rescue a colleague from a plumbing crisis in the Ladies' as she is to change a flat tyre on the way home from work. Little fazes a **4** in a working day, and she is **forever practical** behind her apparently permanent 'Do not disturb' sign. Though she always looks entrenched and busy, she is ready to **help** a new recruit through a difficult day, or find a better deal for a ticket price to an out-of-town conference. In fact, such a task offers a delicious challenge, as she loves to prove that she can still have a hand in the tiniest detail, even when she has climbed the corporate ladder right to the top.

She prides herself on **knowing** what her assistant is worrying about, or understanding that the air-cooling system is down and everyone else's concentration is wandering. **Details** are her business, and those who work for her will quickly discover that a good day for them lies in having the same grasp of such details.

3 2 1 9 8 7 6 5 4

WORK PROFILE
The 4 male boss

He may look smart in the **traditional** sense – a carefully chosen tie (**dignified** rather than flashy), and a suit that shows he spends his money in a proper establishment – but the **4** man in charge is never stuffy. He is **down to earth** and popular, **charming**, and maybe a little old-fashioned – and everyone likes him that way. Newfangled accessories are not required to make business tick along well, but a **good feeling** between associates is definitely a must, and he will spend time making sure everyone knows exactly what they have to do, and go over it again to make sure. If anything is missing he'll take care of it himself, for he is never above **mucking in** with the workers, ready to grab a sandwich at his desk rather than eat out at the chichi restaurant over the road. He is so **reliable** when it comes to finishing his work that he is bound to miss his train home two or three times a week: it comes with the territory.

The **4** male boss fits an astonishing amount into his day. Rather than dashing around madly, he will **pace himself** properly and go the distance for a long, concentrated series of encounters that he undoubtedly set up himself, knowing his own **stamina**. He puts younger colleagues in the shade with his ability to hold on to a long list of client details and business names, and he has the power to keep everyone **calm** with his dry **humour** and enjoyment of a practical joke in heated circumstances. Is there anyone you'd rather work for?

A **4** male boss is proof that the best traditions don't always have to give way. He is **dependable** and **organized**, helps to organize his underlings, and likes to know the details of a case or a problem. And everyone calls him by his first name. It may seem disrespectful – but, at base, the **4** boss is just **one of the team**, and happy to be so.

WORK PROFILE
The 4 female employee

Wearing a suit even in a less formal environment, the **4** female coming to work in her first week or two is a **model of reliability**. No matter if there is a train strike or the bus didn't arrive, she is there on time and has the paperwork she needs for her first ever meeting. Sporting **sensible** flat heels (albeit on quite smart footwear!), she won't lose a number or an address, and never forgets what time her boss likes tea. She is **determined** and **work-orientated**, knowing that life demands a good income and **security** if we are to negotiate it comfortably – and she is very well-disciplined in this respect. She will make sure she is appraised of any fact and every facet of a project, so as not to let the team down.

The **4** female employee is mysterious, in a sense:

everyone sees her as **conservative** and cautious – which she is – and yet there is a **humour bubbling underneath** which makes it a pleasure to get to know her better. As **4** never boasts or brags about its achievements, she has to take her time to tell her co-workers that in her spare time she sculpts, or is doing a catering course, or runs the half-marathon as a sheer expression of physical stamina. She is a **surprise package**, but is a **loyal friend** to anyone who needs a wise listener and is not afraid to 'hear it like it is'.

She is **honest** to the bone, and can't be bothered with absurd niceties. If you ask her a question, you'll get a **straight** answer. 'Why else would you ask me?' she wonders. And why else would you, indeed? She can see things exactly as they are, and is more than happy to tell you. If the rest of us are open to reason and **practical assessment**, the **4** at work is the girl who can tell us everything.

3   2   1   9   8   7   6   5   4

WORK PROFILE
The 4 male employee

Preferring slightly sporty, **hard-wearing** clothes, chosen for comfort and good service without needing dry-cleaning, the young **4** male comes to work with his **mind already on the job**. He may seem a little **unsmiling** in the office meeting — after all, there is a time and place for mirth — but he is **astute** and **up to speed** on all the details he needs to show up anyone who is coasting and not keeping up with the job requirements. For this reason he may make enemies, for he doesn't approve of wasted time and money, or of someone being unfair or not contributing.

With a natural instinct for **streamlining** and maximizing output, he is **on his way up** to deputy head of the firm — deputy, because he's not asking for a high-profile or showy position. However, management soon find they can't do without his **cool head** and his **diligence**. Rain or shine, sickness or health, he reports for work every day unless he is hospitalized. And, if he's laid up in bed, he'll work from home!

The **4** male employee doesn't *mean* to be censorious of others having fun during their working day: in actual fact, in the pub after work, he'll reveal that he's a **brilliant mimic** and has a great sense of **humour** – the more hilarious because no one saw it coming. During the day, though, he's too busy sifting through the pile that has been thrown on his desk in desperation to have fun. He is known as the man for a **last-minute brief**, and he is able to find information at the drop of a hat because he **assiduously** maintains his contacts, and his reference books are within easy reach. Note that his desk is **neatly organized** and he has things carefully labelled. When he is boss (and that day will come), his assistant will have a **hard act to follow**!

Ideal world or cruel world?
Best and worst jobs ...

IN AN IDEAL WORLD

Best job for a 4 female: International funds manager for a highly regarded charity or human rights organization (satisfies the need to do something worthwhile, offers chance to trim away wasted expenditure – a job with a mission!)

Best job for a 4 male: Manager of celebrated botanical gardens or famous nursery (responsible for making money and producing worthy products – and doing gardening for a living!)

IN A CRUEL WORLD

Worst job for a 4 female: Assistant to self-centred Z-list celebrity (having to pander to someone who has nothing of importance to say)

Worst job for a 4 male: Mopping up spills and accidents in a busy hospital (able to face the work, but frustrated at how much more he would like to contribute)

4'S CHILDHOOD

**Seeing the way a number expresses itself in someone
very young is fascinating, for the tendencies and
responses are all in their infancy – and yet plain to
see. Some facets of a number's power need to be
grown into, and take time to reveal how they will be
dealt with by the developing character. Sometimes
the strength of a number can be a frustration
when we're young.**

If looking back on your own childhood through the lens
of your number, you should discover – with considerable
humour and irony – a renewed understanding of some of
the difficulties or excitements you experienced. Or, if you
have a child who is also a **4**, you may learn something more
useful; it is an advantage to understand the qualities a

number exudes over an awakening personality, especially in relation to talents and career strengths, as it might save a lot of frustrations. You'll be able to appreciate the positive traits, and handle negative ones more sympathetically.

Here, we take a detailed look at what it's like to be a child bearing your number. But what about the other numbers? Perhaps you have a child who is a **7**, and you'd like to know what that means? Or maybe you'd like to gain insight into friends' and siblings' childhoods, to see if it sheds any light on the people they have become today? A short profile is given for each number, along with advice for a **4** parent on dealing with other-number offspring.

Just as your own parents would have discovered when you yourself were a child, the hardest thing with a **4** child is encouraging their care and hard work in what interests them, but at the same time dissuading them from stubbornness, or their disinclination to try new things. **4** has a mind all of its own, and childhood is no exception ...

4 5 6 7 8 9 1 2 3

The young 4

A child born on the 4th, 13th, 22nd or 31st is an intense little character for any parent to deal with. It is of the utmost importance to help them feel secure and confident, for **4**s worry even as children about getting all the information they need, or having all the equipment for an outing, or making sure all the details are right for a first day of a new term. **4** doesn't like to make mistakes. Part of a **4** child's interest in saving up for cherished possessions or hoarding what is given to them for birthdays is about feeling more secure: solid objects can be measured, whereas ideas cannot.

As children, **4**s begin to learn the merits of being organized, and, unless there are some strange complications in their birth-date numbers, or they lack a letter in their name to back up their **4** nature, they should be tidy in their rooms and will prefer clean clothes. A **4** child will be readier than most to help with the dishes or hang up their things; but they can be very possessive of their own belongings, too, and may resent siblings 'borrowing' from time to time. **4** always likes to put a box around something – in this case, their material goods and their space!

Although they are not exactly tearaways, **4** children are physically stoical and like to concentrate their energies on sporty pursuits or physical challenges. Their temperament suits camping out, climbing hills and trees, or exploring old houses. This is not because they have that insatiable curiosity that fuels **1**s and **5**s, but because they like to understand how things are done and what happens in various situations, and they like the challenge of a little bit of hardship. You might just say that **4**s are tough and quite brave.

If a **4** child is given a corner of the garden, don't be surprised if they nurture it with maturity and competence.

4's toys

Children's encyclopedia • Books • Lego set • Microscope or telescope • Cricket bat or tennis racket • Colouring pencils • Pick-up sticks • Child's gardening tools • Child's cookery book • Embroidery supplies • Jewellery kit

They love to grow vegetables alongside flowers, and to be given their own quiet authority to design their space, so that they can work out the most productive or useful arrangement. They also enjoy contributing to the building of playhouses or climbing equipment.

All **4**s need strong family relationships when they are young, and need to be trusted with their own authority in some tasks. They are naturally cautious anyhow, and unlikely to get themselves into serious dramas, preferring, in fact, to observe their friends getting cuts and grazes, and to learn — from watching others in this way — not to replicate the pain. **4**s are also less likely than most children to pledge their trust to anyone else unless it is earned.

But, what a hard worker and focused child this should be – willing to put in the hours of practice to play an instrument or a sport, ready to memorize times tables and spelling lists, and generally very occupied with mind-absorbing interests like reading and computer games. They love to earn pocket money and will help with virtually any household chore to this gain, so – well directed – this may be a dream child for most parents. And, if you are a **4** parent with a **4** child, you should respect each other most of the time, even though you will often lock your stubborn horns together.

The young master number 22

If the **4** in question was born on the 22nd, you will discover a child with a high level of intuition and observation

— as well as healthy scepticism. The **22** child is in a hurry to be an adult, to be taken seriously, and to make a difference in the world. **22** boys and girls almost enjoy escaping from difficult situations, so don't be surprised if they deliberately put themselves through some stress just to find out how to land on their feet again. Highly intelligent, and possessing a developed sense of the geography of the world, **22** children are impatient with the slower minds of their contemporaries, and may seek the company of adults. But one thing's for sure: they are headed somewhere different to the crowd.

The 1 child

This resourceful child has a different way of thinking, and will stand to one side and evaluate things without pressure. Repeat Grandma's sound advice on any subject to a **1** under the age of six, and they'll simply ask, 'Why?' Ignoring the social expectation to conform, **1** children often make us laugh with surprise.

A **1** child is tough and active – an inquisitive soul who wants to get on with things and not be held in check by others, however wise the parental eye might be. Stubborn and impatient, **1**s frequently suffer by questioning – though not from rudeness – the authority of a parent or teacher. **1**s break down tradition and find new ideas to form a fresh understanding of the world we're in. Your **1** child needs careful handling: a bright mind bursting with interest and disinclined to authority needs subtle direction. If **1** children dominate their friends and talk over their family it can make them socially inept and unable to co-operate in love relationships later in life, leading to loneliness rather than just self-reliance.

A **1**'s greatest challenge is to learn to live in a social world and understand that they are not inevitably right. To foster a **1**'s unique personality and avoid insensitivity to others, let them behave like an adult. This confidence a **1** child will ably repay. **1** children suffer from being misunderstood, as they're often so happy in their private hours and so demanding of having their own time that they may not learn to express their need for others. The seeds are sown early as to how to approach another person for signs of affection, and a **4** parent knows how to wait for a **1** child to ask them something, as well as granting them their needed sense of privacy. Try, at times, to hug them solidly: **1** will relish such a respectful approach – as long as you're not too demanding about how they conduct themselves.

The 2 child

All children born on the 2nd or 20th need affection and a peaceful environment to grow up in. Those born on the 11th or 29th are a little different, being master number **11**s with **2** as the denominator, and they have an old head on young shoulders from the beginning of their lives. But even they – for all their drive toward excitement and adventure – will be happiest if their home life is mostly secure and tranquil.

These highly sensitive and intuitive children know what you will say before you say it. They are also dreamy and process ideas in their sleep, waking to instinctive and wise solutions to their problems. But they are vulnerable, and need reassuring more than most numbers. They are acutely sensitive to criticism, feeling that all comments are proof that they're not quite good enough, so you need to deliver your words with tact and an awareness of their needs.

2 children are talented artists, actors, dancers and/or musicians: they know how others *feel*. A **2** child prefers to support friends and family as often as possible, and this can make them a doormat ready to be walked on unless those they live with are alert to their inclinations. If the **2** is an **11**, the wish to help out will be very strong indeed, but these children also have a finely tuned moral sense and will be offended by injustice – especially against them! Don't dish out judgement until you have all the facts.

2s are good healers and can make others feel better. Knowing when to cuddle or touch and when to be quiet, they often have a stillness which works miracles around the sick, the sad and the elderly. A **4** parent of a **2** will bolster their confidence and make them feel securely loved, giving them a quiet space for their inner calm. **2** has a similar need for teamwork – but **4** expects results, and must let them find their own way through. Overall, you should have an excellent bond with your gentle, intelligent **2**.

The 3 child

From the cradle, **3**s hold parties and like to mix with other children. They have a capacity to laugh and precipitate laughter, even when things go a little wrong. **3** children are like the reappearing sun after rain, and their energies can be restorative for everyone. Creative and playful, nothing keeps them low for long.

Like a juggler keeping plates and balls in the air, **3**s have several activities and talents on the go from the start. This can be a problem, however: making decisions is hard for them, and they need a wise older counsellor who can talk out the options and give them room to think. Even then, a decision once reached can always be changed – and a **3** child will find a way to run in several directions at one time.

Keep your **3** busy with lots of artistic activities, using colours and textures – right from babyhood – to open their eyes to what they can do. Even before the age of ten, a strong personal taste will begin to develop – and it may not be the same as their parents'. Using up their flow of energy on a multitude of tasks will be demanding on both parents, but the **3** child does give a great deal back in return.

3s are talkers and have a witty repartee, even when tiny: you'll be surprised at what you hear from them sometimes, and will wonder where it came from. Naturally gifted at PR, they will talk you around when you are set against one of their wishes, but you will need to direct them now and again or nothing will ever be finished! A **4** parent with a **3** child must allow them scope to try things differently (which they will do), and not be upset if they are sometimes messy or chatter too much, disturbing **4**'s routine. Just draw clear lines for your **3** to follow, and they will always come up smiling.

3 2 1 9 8 7 6 5 4

The 5 child

Unable to be confined or to sit still, a **5** child is bursting with curiosity about life and people. Very sociable and happy to be on the move, these adventurous youngsters have much in common with **1**s, but are more willing to work in a team, and good at picking up on other people's ideas, only to improve them.

From their first few words, **5** children have good memories and a facility for speech – they speak and learn quickly, and can pick up more than one language. Even more physical than 1s (although the two numbers are alike in this), they are excellent at sport or physical co-ordination. They chatter, are full of energy, and like to play to an audience. But most importantly, **5** children love to be free – to explore, laze, hunt, create, discover and travel. Take your **5** child away on holiday and they quickly make friends with others, and acquire a taste for foreign places. They will even experiment with different food, if you're lucky.

5s find a reason to slip away if they're bored with adult company – so don't be offended. Their minds can pursue several streams of active interest, so they need a great deal of amusement to stretch them. This adventurous spirit can be a worry to their family sometimes and, indeed, **5**s need to understand house rules about asking first, or telling someone where they're off to. The difficulty is that **5** children usually don't want to explain themselves to anyone.

The test for a **5**'s parent is to set their child constructive challenges that will vent their curiosity in good ways. **5**s will pick up technology and music (other forms of language, in a sense) quickly, but they don't like dull routine work – which will irritate a **4** sibling if they have one. A **4** parent of a **5** child results in a confrontation of styles – older/younger, traditional/modern – and arguments about freedom to roam may be a particular problem for you!

3 2 1 9 8 7 6 5 4

The 6 child

Here's a young soul in need of a peaceful haven, just like a
2, but a **6** will literally feel ill if there is dissension around
them. Always wanting to beautify their surroundings and
make pretty presents for Mum, these talented, sensitive
children have many gifts for creative expression. They will
also nurse the sick cat or anyone who needs gentle kindness, but are not always robust themselves, and should be
sheltered from bad weather or aggressive viruses.

As children, **6**'s musical talents should emerge – and
they often have beautiful speaking or singing voices. They
are also the peacemakers of the family – natural creators
of balance and harmony. Give them a free hand with their
bedroom and their flower garden, and be ready to learn
from them. Both boys and girls usually make good cooks
when they are older, too, so time spent in the kitchen won't

be wasted. Birthday presents that foster their good eye — a camera or set of art tools — will usually fit them well.

Despite being sensitive to others and quite intuitive, **6** as a child is a little shy and needs drawing out — especially if there has been much change in their young life, because **6** children need stability and like to remain a tiny bit traditional. They become very attached to their home. But if their family life is unconventional they will ultimately adjust, because they offer their family a lot of love, and like to be shown love in return. Even the boys have a feminine side, which in no way calls their gender into question.

Good at school and almost as well-organized as **4**s, this is a number which needs time to grow into itself: **6**s really are enormously talented. A **4** parent shares their **6** child's love of security and thinking space, but must allow them to work their own way. When you need a friend to listen, support, encourage and back *you* up, you will often find unsuspected reservoirs of strength in this interesting child.

The 7 child

Even in primary school this is a child with a focused mind and a strongly developed critical sense. A **7** child is perceptive and, sometimes, disarmingly quiet. They will often prefer adult company, as their peers will probably seem too young and underdeveloped to them. Wise and difficult to know well, these are children with a serious cast to their intelligent minds.

The fact that a **7** child can sit quietly and contemplate things deeply should not imply that they are introverted: quite the opposite. A **7** will grow into a very good host as long as the company appeals, and they have a lovely sense of humour, apparent from their earliest years – even if it does sometimes find expression at others' expense. They will rarely be rude, but certainly have a good understanding of all that has been said – and what has not been.

Listen to their impressions of the people they deal with!

All **7**s as children have an inward reluctance to accept other people's ideas automatically – rather like **1**s – but there is a special propensity to independence in a child born on the 16th. This is the number of someone who finds it difficult asking for what they want – someone who often feels as though they haven't been consulted as to their own wishes. And all **7**s certainly have definite ideas about what to believe.

7 children should be told the truth on virtually all matters; they will know if they are being deceived, and will respect being treated as an adult in any case. A **4** parent may find their reserve and maturity admirable, and will respect their **7** child's strength. Though different – a **7** child keen to retire into even more privacy and personal space – these two numbers are not dissimilar, and a **7** child gives any parent much to be proud of, both academically and in terms of humanitarian feelings.

3   2   1   9   8   7   6   5   4

The 8 child

Here we have a young executive in the making. Even when they are still at school these children have a canny nose for what will make good business — and yet they are generous, hard-working and prepared to learn everything it will take to succeed in this life. Children born on the 8th, 17th and 26th like to have charge of their own finances, and to be given scope to do 'grown-up' activities — organizing their own parties and making arrangements for outings with their friends.

These children have strength and energy, but mentally are reflective and wise, too. They always see both sides to an argument — so parents who ask them to choose sides, beware! An **8** makes good judgements, and even before the age of ten they have a sense of what is fair and what is morally right.

4   5   6   7   8   9   1   2   3

As this number rules the octave, many **8** children are extremely musical and have a wonderful sense of rhythm. This last even assures they can be good at sport, as it takes innate timing to perfect many physical skills. **8**s also like philosophical ideas and relish being given 'big concepts' to chew over, especially concerning politics or religious ideas. **8**s are proud, and like to research things carefully — so as long as they are not bored, you will find an **8** child with their head in a book or on the internet, or watching programmes that educate and broaden their vistas.

An **8** child is always striving for balance, and you must be pragmatic if they are sometimes pulling in the opposite direction from you. **8**s are loyal to those they love, but a delicate sensibility makes them look at the other side of a story, or fight for an underdog. As a **4**, you understand this urge to make a difference well, and mostly you will respect the qualities and mind of your **8** child, who is as generous materially.

3 2 1 9 8 7 6 5 4

The 9 child

Here is a person born for the theatre, or to travel the world and befriend everyone. **9**s have an expansive view of things, and don't like to be restricted. With a good head for both science and the arts, there are many career directions open, so parents will have their work cut out trying to help them choose. However, because the number **9** is like a mirror, with every number added to it reducing again to that same number (for example: 5+9 = 14, and 1+4 = 5), **9** children are able to take on the feelings of just about anyone, which is why they are so artistic and good at drama and writing.

From their first years in school it will be clear a **9** child has a wonderful dry sense of humour and a taste for the unusual. **9** children are not often prejudiced and seem to be easy-going – though they are sensitive to the atmosphere around them, picking up vibes like a sponge. If you speak to them harshly they will take it seriously, and are protective of others who seem to be hurt in this way too.

9s have a delicate relationship with their parents, but particularly with the father figure. A **9** girl will want to idolize her dad, and will feel desperately disappointed if circumstances are against this, while a **9** boy may wish to emulate his father – and yet they often grow up without enough input from this important person, who is busy or away. A **9** child must be wise ahead of their time, and so this lesson is thrown at them in one guise or another.

The **4** parent of a **9** child understands very well how to cultivate their gifts, though may want them to focus more and work harder. Your **9** child appreciates your patience and the secure home you give them, but wants to explore the outer world too. **9** equally recognizes your wish to provide all they need to grow, and will reward you with affection and kindness. Grown-ups from the start, their honesty and willingness to keep the peace fill you with admiration.

| 3 | 2 | 1 | 9 | 8 | 7 | 6 | 5 | 4 |

4 AT PLAY

We have discovered how your number expresses itself through your character in relation to your family and your general personality, what instinctive reactions go with your number in everyday situations, and how it might shape your career path and colour your childhood. But every day our DAY number also influences the way we respond to the social world around us. So, what can it say about our leisure hours? Is yours a number that even allows itself to relax? (Well, you probably already have some answers to this one!) What can your number reveal about the way you like to spend your time, or how you achieve pleasure outside of duty?

4   5   6   7   8   9   1   2   3

Over the next few pages we take a look at what makes you tick, as a **4**, when you are unwinding – and how **4**s prefer to fill their time, if given a choice. Let's see whether you're typical in this respect ... And who knows – if you haven't already tried all the activities and pastimes mentioned, maybe you'll get a few ideas about what to put on your list for next time!

The 4 woman at play

To this point, you will have seen a pattern that tells us **4** is a number which relishes form and the creation of something solid, rather than just an idea. And so it is with leisure time. You are happiest working on anything that presents a finished product at the end. Unafraid of social comment, and disregarding the 'traditional' male/female divide, you are perfectly comfortable wielding your power drill, sanding woodwork, and tiling to your heart's content ...

But are we talking about work or leisure time here? This is at the hub of **4**'s character, and, for a **4** woman, this kind of work is a hobby. Getting something done is a joy! A satisfying weekend will see a garden room installed, new locks put on the doors and a renovated bathroom. Such an achievement is a delight for a **4**, and a week off could see a radical alteration to the whole house or garden.

4   5   6   7   8   9   1   2   3

Leisure for you is not idle. Days off will be a delight when something is done: perhaps a visit to a place you've never been – somewhere where you may learn something. Weekend courses in cake decorating, stained-glass-window making, woodwork ... all will prove satisfying methods of relaxation. Overalls very likely form part of your wardrobe, and you will always get your hands dirty clearing out the undergrowth by the far wall in the garden. If you break a nail (enough to horrify a **2**!), it will grow again.

This doesn't mean away-time is excluded, for travel has a strong appeal. Happiest trips would include a place to go biking or hiking, or, if tranquillity is what you're after, a garden is a must. The outdoors is **4**'s domain, for, although form and order are vital to your security, being boxed in is not part of the plan in your leisure time. The earth – its smell and feel, even its taste – is an essential part of your recreation, and many happy leisure hours are spent marking out your turf. If a **4** woman doesn't have a garden, something truly significant is missing in her life.

4 women are very earthy and refreshingly gritty about their relationships, and there's no doubt that leisure hours spent with your lover are a priority. Not necessarily demanding luxurious or romantic locations to put you in the mood, you can recharge your batteries just walking with your loved one near the sea, or curl up reading a book in a hammock with your lover nearby. Neither cloying nor whiny, you are practical about love relationships, and strolling on the beach for an hour in the evening on a long hot day can be the best leisure time there is for a smart and loyal female **4**.

Favourite holiday destinations for a **4** to escape to in a free week include the rough and mountainous terrains that characterize some of the Greek mainland and Spain. Camping in the Rockies would have its allure, as would a sailing holiday which demands that passengers become part of the crew. While you're not the female equivalent of

Action Man, you do like to have something to do, rather than just having thinking time; getting a tan or shopping is not an end in itself for you. Joining friends or entertaining are activities which bring you happiness, but one-on-one is best – just a few close people, or family. This always means the most to **4**s. And an experience weekend is more likely to hit the spot if it invites you to take part in an archaeological dig or a wine-tasting course than the less strenuous activity of spa or beauty treatments. Simply, you can relax more when something is happening gently.

Hobby skills? We have said that any time spent honing the talents you have with your hands will be a pleasure. So, many **4** women are good at needlepoint, icing cakes, painting detailed miniatures or murals on walls, making jewellery, playing the piano. What stands out about a **4**'s talent in these areas is that you use your head to execute these skills, rather than your heart. The result is, thus, often much better for it!

The 4 man at play

For a number that is renowned for pacing itself in all activities and subsequently getting through the most arduous tasks, 'rush! rush!' is not how a **4** man will enjoy his own time. Leisure hours for you are varied, and will surprise many as to their make-up, but quality time which allows for thought and focused enjoyment is a part of the demand. You can be at leisure just having time to read the Sunday paper from cover to cover in your own garden. It's not essential to go away somewhere, or hurry across the landscape visiting others from dawn till dusk. Family time, or a day spent talking quietly with your partner, is as much a part of a **4** at play as anything else.

A **4** man also likes his power tools and garden equipment. Just like the **4** girl next door, any hours that tick gently by while a room is painted, a barbecue built or a new kitchen fitted will make you feel your time was well spent. You're no slouch with a drill or saw, either, for **4** is the number of the carpenter and the builder, remember, and this is a pleasure for most **4** men rather than a chore. You can sit down afterwards with a glass of something nice and admire your handiwork.

When you hit the trail you are happiest if your time away isn't *completely* self-indulgent. A trip that combines family duty or visiting friends, or a week in a villa improving a language, will be the best use of your play time. And you will give of yourself quite generously, too, always ready to help with a local hospital fête or school play, or setting up new music or computer equipment for your children or a technophobic uncle. It is always in **4**'s mind to be of help and of use, and doing so represents pleasure time.

But lest we make **4** chaps sound like the all-working Jack who becomes dull, they can be very content going to the opera or to a play, sitting on a porch with a good book or messing about on a river. It is the quietude that counts here, and the kind of stimulus that makes this intelligent fellow think more deeply. You are focused rather than giddy, and the hours that are your own should be about some kind of challenge to yourself – whether that is mounted in a camping trip or a trip to the movies (and always best, of course, with family or one or two close friends).

Other leisure interests likely to appeal to a **4** gentleman might leave other numbers wondering. You will be amused gong to a weekend lecture or spending time on a golf course, just to get your brain clear; you can be in your element fishing (far too quiet for a **3** or a **5** male friend!); and you can even find enjoyment going through your accounts or that box of documents in the corner (can this be possible?). Laundering your clothes or organizing the sock drawer could reveal untold hours of happiness. These things are to a purpose, and they remove the cobwebs from your mind, allowing you to relax and unwind in ways that make no sense to human beings who aren't as *still* as you. It is a thing of beauty for a **4** to have a truly clean house, and even a **4** man finds pleasure in the creating of one.

But what of your hobby time? What activities raise your pulse? Strangely, under the bonnet of your car you are a gifted mechanic, just as you can be an excellent drummer or short-story writer. You have such a solid grasp of life that you are able to project your thoughts into other people's minds and activities without losing yourself in the process. **4** men, therefore, are often performers in a quiet way, sharing themselves with those who know them well, if not a crowd. You will be a good writer or painter as a result of focusing on what makes other people tick – a creativity born of close observation rather than wild leaps of imagination. And such careful analysis gives you pleasure.

4 IN LOVE

Love: it's what we all want to know about. What's your style as a lover? And your taste — where does that run? Do you want a partner who is, ideally, more sociable and flamboyant than you? Or would you rather have a love in your life who is happy to take a quieter role with you, so that you both shine equally together, discovering each other at your own pace rather than filling your time with other people to distract you from your relationship? Everything about you screams 'reliability', but is this all there is to your love life?

Our first task is to consider how you see others as potential partners, and what you are likely to need from them. Why are you attracted to someone in the first place? This is where we begin ... But then you might like to pass the book across to your other half (if you have one), for the second subject of discussion is: why are *they* attracted to *you*? What does it mean to have a **4** lover?

Telltale traits of the 4 lover

- Serious intentions
- Earthy about physical attraction
- Open and honest – and wants this to be reciprocated by their partner
- Cautious about too much overt expression
- Needs to respect their lover
- Intelligent, and looks for this in others
- Likes someone to talk closely with

How do you do?
A 4 IN ATTRACTION

4s are attracted to people whose very demeanour says 'classy'. Whether you're a boy or girl, young or old, let's face it: you like quality. You will be drawn to the best partner you can find on the market. This sounds calculating, but it is really testament to your innate respect for someone who exudes poise and dignity, and shows they are well mannered and well-informed.

4s are never convinced by boisterous and noisy partners who attract the populace at large. You aren't looking to go out with a show pony, but much prefer a thoroughbred who will be comfortable in every situation. You don't like to make a big splash yourself, and the idea of being involved closely with anyone who is too overt or flashy is not an option for more than a brief glance. Without being

| 4 | 5 | 6 | 7 | 8 | 9 | 1 | 2 | 3 |

a prude, you have a high sense of what is morally right, and a relationship must be built with someone who can live up to this ideal. A partner can be sexy, a high achiever, determined – but never blond and silly. You are attracted to a potential lover because of their mind and their quiet good style.

You shine for others who are also attracted by a good brain and humour that is meant for one discerning ear rather than a room full of people. 4s in love are like a good-quality perfume: they emit a subtle but compelling signal to someone special who is both in range and of a particular ilk, rather than spreading an overpowering aroma across a entire dance floor (that reaches even the bouncers outside!). 4 is a byword for subtlety and discretion, and those who are drawn to people who are charismatic but lack substance will completely miss the classier appearance and character of a 4. For someone of such solid worth and intelligence, you are often lacking in the self-confidence department, and it takes a very special person to over-come that shyness and get to the delightful business of knowing you well.

Go easy!

When you feel a strong pull to another person, one thing's for sure: you won't have given your affection lightly. However, when you are experiencing the first pangs of love, it's important that you go gently into the second phase of attraction. You don't much like being contradicted and can be very stubborn, so it may be necessary to give a new love room to express themselves, so you can find out what they feel too, before asserting your own opinion too strongly. Potential relationships can be nipped in the bud by such signals, and, although everything would be fine if you could skip the courtship stage and proceed straight to the bit you do best (the reliable and loyal ongoing lover), getting over the introductions could spell the end of the relationship if you don't loosen up just a touch until you both become close.

You like to be in control of what is happening, but this can be suffocating to someone who is unused to your caring personality; in actual fact, you're simply trying to make things feel secure. There will come the day when that trait is the most desirable in a relationship – but tread softly at the start!

Love is for life

Once a relationship is under way, you love with sincerity. It may be that no one quite measures up to a past love, or that the person who is the longest love in your life is never fully replaced, should that bond come to an end for any reason. You like to nest for life. You're a great catch, as you love the simple pleasures in life, and are blind to any lack of quality in others that you feel is only cosmetic. You enjoy good food and spending time with your family, and are willing to share your time appeasing this need in a partner, too.

Responsibility is something you take seriously, and it doesn't stop with the people you are related to. You are amazingly patient, even indulgent, with all the people who have a place in your heart. To a potential partner, a **4**'s willingness to satisfy their partner's family demands may seem saintly! It will definitely be a plus for a loved one who has familial obligations of their own, for a relationship with a **4** is a relationship that implicitly includes burden-sharing.

The people who will love a **4** most are those who have been hurt or let down, or who feel that their own upbringing was lacking in security. You want nothing better than to put your arms around your love, and stand strong though the wind blows. For anyone who has never enjoyed this sense of back-up, such a powerful emotional ally will be the love of their life. You offer this. Relationships are not transient things for you. The word 'fling' is virtually absent from your vocabulary.

You can be a lot of fun, good-natured, quite generous, hard-working and have a dry humour; but love relationships are not to be toyed with. You want someone with whom to co-operate and build a life, and when you have found that person, little can dissuade you from settling — even if all the world should oppose it. Once your mind is made up in love, it's unshakeable. This means that if any heart, however reluctant, can be won through scaling the battlements and ploughing the fields in a storm, **4** will win. Nothing will turn you away if your heart is truly given.

To have and to hold?

LOVING A NUMBER 4

Are you are in love with a **4**? You may even have won their heart, but it could be some time before you recognize this, because **4** gives its heart away cautiously. All **4**s want to be sure their love is the real deal before surrendering their emotions, because, first and last, they are looking for someone very unique, patient and clever. A **4** is never going to be in love with a pole dancer or a Chippendale: no matter how great the physical attraction, such light-headedness won't suit the serious cast of their mind. And, morally, a **4** has to respect whoever they love. The new boy at work will never win the heart of the smart **4** girl in accounts by cracking jokes and wearing peacock colours. She may take notice, though, if he gives her a little room, then invites her to a quiet, old-fashioned restaurant – and has something important to talk about. She likes to have fun, but not giddy fun. **4**s are discerning about those they want to get close to.

If you want to win the heart of this fine, understated character, flirting with other people will get you erased from their phone book rather than noticed. You need to be patient in getting to know them, and you must be sure that their stubbornness is something you can live with – because it isn't going to go away. **4**s in love like to think in their own time and way, and no amount of sales chat from others or wheedling from suitors will make a jot of difference. A **4** will give their affection when and where they deem it earned and merited.

So why would you love such an intractable customer? What is it about **4** that is so desirable? Well, for starters, everything about a **4** – male or female – is a little out of the ordinary. If a **4** becomes engaged in a cause or a task they believe in, they will go out on a limb for you over it. Their careful, intelligent mind impresses, and the very fact that they are not won over by the latest modern must-have item is a cause for humour and admiration from others. You know your **4** is going somewhere, and though a life with a **4** partner might not be lived in the absolute lap of luxury, neither will it be too modest. **4** is sensible about providing, and works hard to secure a dream that their partner is willing to subscribe to. No one will try harder for you.

What's the hurry?

Don't hurry your **4** lover – about anything. Sometimes you must pop an idea gently into their mind and let it filter through for a few days before you get a result. A **4** may work slowly and carefully, but better results come from this, and your relationship is more likely to blossom if you seem to have your own feet on the ground, your own life to live, while your **4** is busy with their own agenda. Finding just the right blend of independence and co-operation is what makes a bond with a **4** work well. And anyone who loves a **4** will smile wryly as they amass more financial security and working respect from their community than more impulsive and imaginative people around them, who start off well only to dissipate what they gained so quickly.

So, if you're in love with a **4** and want to know how to move things into the realm of permanence, give it time and do something fruitful yourself. A **4** will be more in love with someone they can look at as an equal, rather than up to. **4** admires a disciplined mind and a well-thought-out career path in a partner. And your **4** won't go off you if you put on a few pounds or gain a wrinkle or two; they give their love for better or worse, and, as long as the one they love doesn't become dull and disinterested in what the **4** is doing, there should be an excellent chance of ongoing happiness for years. **4**, after all, hasn't changed in what they were looking for. As long as you stay true and focused, life should be better than fine for both of you.

3 2 1 9 8 7 6 5 4

4 in love

Turn-ons:

- ♥ ✔ A partner with a sharp mind and a sunny attitude in the face of a test
- ♥ ✔ Someone who wants to hear what they have to say (not just what they want to wear!)
- ♥ ✔ A focused thinker with a dry sense of humour
- ♥ ✔ A good conversationalist (an absolute must!)

Turn-offs:

- ♥ ✘ Someone who is uninformed or lazy
- ♥ ✘ A constant chatterer, egotist or self-publicist
- ♥ ✘ A lover with a completely self-absorbed outlook
- ♥ ✘ A partner who tries to change you (they'll be heading for trouble!)

4'S COMPATIBILITY

In this weighty section you have the tools to find
out how well you click with all the other numbers
in matters of the heart, but also when you have to
work or play together too. Each category opens with
a star-ratings chart, showing you – at a glance –
whether you're going to encounter plain sailing or
stormy waters in any given relationship. First up is
love: if your number matches up especially well with
the person you're with, you will appreciate why
certain facets of your bond just seem to slot
together easily.

But, of course, we're not always attracted to the people
who make the easiest relationships for us, and if you find
that the one you love rates only one or two stars, don't

3   2   1   9   8   7   6   5   4

give in! Challenges are often the 'meat' of a love affair —
and all difficulties are somewhat soothed if you both share
a birthday number in common, even if that number is
derived from the *total* of the birth date rather than the
actual **DAY** number. In other words, if your partner's **LIFE**
number is the same as your **DAY** number, you will feel a
pull towards each other which is very strong, even if the
DAY numbers taken together have some wrinkles in their
match-up. You will read more about this in the pages that
follow the star chart.

The charts also include the master numbers **11** and
22: these bring an extra dimension to relationships for
those whose birth-number calculations feature either of
these numbers at any stage. (For example, someone with
a **DAY** number of **2** may be born on the 29th: 2+9 = **11**,
and 1+1 = **2**. This means you should read the compatibility pairings for your number with both a **2** and an **11**.)

Sometimes the tensions that come to the surface in

4   5   6   7   8   9   1   2   3

love relationships are excellent for business relationships instead: the competitiveness that can undermine personal ties can accelerate effectiveness in working situations. We'll take a look at how other numbers match up with yours in vocational situations. And, when it comes to friends, you'll see why not all of your friendships are necessarily a smooth ride ...

In all matters – whether love, work or friendship – you will probably discover that the best partnerships you make involve an overlap of at least one number that you share in common. A number **4** attracts other number **4**s in various close ties throughout life.

NOTE: To satisfy your curiosity, **ALL** numbers are included in the star charts, so that you can check the compatibility ratings between your friends, co-workers and loved ones – and see why some relationships may be more turbulent than others!

3 2 1 9 8 7 6 5 4

Love

YOUR **LOVE** COMPATIBILITY CHART

	1	2	3	4	5
With a 1	★★★★	★★★★★	★★	★★★	★★★★★
With a 2	★★★★★	★★★★	★★★	★★★★★	★
With a 3	★★	★★★	★★★★★	★★	★★★★
With a 4	★★★	★★★★★	★★	★★★★	★★
With a 5	★★★★★	★	★★★★	★★	★★★
With a 6	★★★	★★★★	★★★★	★★★	★★
With a 7	★★★★★	★★	★★★	★★★★★	★★★
With an 8	★★★★	★★★★	★★★★★	★★★	★★★
With a 9	★★★	★★★	★★★★★	★★	★★★
With an 11	★★★★	★★★★	★★	★★★★★	★★
With a 22	★★★★	★★★★★	★★★	★★★★	★★★★

4	5	6	7	8	9	1	2	3

6	7	8	9	11	22
★★★	★★★★★	★★★★	★★★	★★★★	★★★★
★★★★	★★	★★★★	★★★	★★★★	★★★★★
★★★★	★★★	★★★★★	★★★★★	★★	★★★
★★★	★★★★★	★★★	★★	★★★★★	★★★★
★★	★★★	★★★	★★★	★★	★★★★
★★★★★	★	★★★	★★★★★	★★★★	★★★★
★	★★★	★★★★	★★★	★★★★	★★★★★
★★★	★★★★	★★★	★★	★★★★★	★★★★
★★★★★	★★★	★★	★★★	★★★★	★★★
★★★★	★★★★	★★★★★	★★★★	★★	★★★★★
★★★★	★★★★★	★★★★	★★★	★★★★★	★★

| 3 | 2 | 1 | 9 | 8 | 7 | 6 | 5 | 4 |

4 in love with a 1   ★★★

As long as you are content being told what to do, this partnership probably has a better chance of succeeding than people would think. On the face of it, you seem so pedantic to many people that you might really annoy a **1**'s creative spirit, and stop them in mid-flow with issues about practicality. However, in practice, you are just the kind of person to help **1** achieve their goals, being the hard worker and one person who will stand up to **1** about the need for proper foundations and good organization.

4s are very often practical to the exclusion of creative interests — but this is not always so, and if you are one of the creative ones, so much the better (this will be truest if you were born on the 22nd or 31st). **4**s are always clever with their hands, and this often manifests as artistic or musical skill, which will have a magnetic appeal for origi-

| 4 | 5 | 6 | 7 | 8 | 9 | 1 | 2 | 3 |

nal **1**. Your **1** also appreciates the way you really listen to them, taking them seriously when others sometimes don't hear them at all. The problem with this is that it seems to be love based on friendship rather than on passion or powerful attraction. Ask yourself this: are you with your **1** because you are useful to them, or because they simply depend on you? If so, you need to work on the problem of your **1** being too self-absorbed and (possibly) selfish to see what you need.

In day-to-day affairs **1** will be the decision-maker, for they always take the lead, and you won't challenge that. What can work very well is that you won't always let impetuous **1** rush into things without thinking it through – restraining their impulsiveness at times when it may be a good to thing to restrain it! You see dangers that **1** doesn't see; and, while they often find this annoying, it is pragmatic and may be of long-term help.

You love **1**'s originality and sense of destiny about life, for things are rarely so glamorous in a **4**'s more carefully planned life. But **4** can sometimes be dull, or forced to feel over-attached to the past, family and routine, and this will discourage **1** from their natural drive to push forwards and try new things. This becomes more than a mere annoyance if your cautious nature blunts **1**'s genuine wit and imagination. This will certainly create friction, and getting around this basic personality difference will be very challenging.

On the positive side, however, you are a willing accomplice who can steady **1** through storms and windy weather emotionally, and your thoroughness – though so different from **1**'s much more explosive bluff – can actually make the **1** you love into a wiser and more productive person. This is why it is good for business (*see also page 182*), and why so many **1**-and-**4** couples do work together, and often from home.

But be wary of something you may not, at first, see. **1** and **4** both have very strong opinions, and **4** needs security in a relationship. If the **1** doesn't identify this need, you will always be pulling against each other, because your natural inclination is to keep your emotions to yourselves. You are serious about life, and need your **1** to try to be so too.

Key themes

Shared love of family · Comfortable home with material trappings · Need to balance impatience of **1** with extreme patience of **4** · Enjoyment of garden and green places · **1** not to 'order' **4** around

4 in love with a 2   ★★★★★

In this five-star relationship, **4** understands just how important it is for **2** to have someone to listen to them. You are **2**'s willing audience, and respect their gentle but wise head on a vast number of subjects. You have the kind of attention to detail that **2** admires, and as lovers you have a willingness to be close and confidential with one another, which builds harmony over time. You may not swing from chandeliers or host wild parties, but you have a mutual respect for people and moral fellow-feeling which makes you attract just the friends and business partners you need to make a solid, peaceful relationship together. Moreover, you really love your **2**: it is a sincere attraction of spirit for spirit, and **2** has the power to influence you to become more affectionate and less utilitarian about life. **2** injects beauty and emotion into **4**'s carefully laid out garden.

4	5	6	7	8	9	1	2	3

Although there is very little friction between you, stubbornness may be the one thorn in the rose bed. 4 stands its ground like no other number, and, if 2 feels strongly about what is at stake, there may be trouble ahead. But this is a minor point, for really 2 and 4 bring out the very best in each other. You not only indulge 2's dreams, but help to make them into realities; and 2 dreams such beautiful dreams, to your mind. 4s are not uncreative, but are often undeveloped artistically because of the need to have lived a very practical and dutiful life. 2 ends all this for you, and encourages your abilities in other areas. You love to place your energies into your home and family, and 2 will never complain about this preference.

So good is the understanding between these numbers that it would suit a relationship that spills into the workplace – or you may both work in a related field. Canny 2 knows when overworking 4 needs to stop and clear their head; and you will always appreciate 2's excellent insights.

3 2 1 9 8 7 6 5 4

You will also rely upon – rather than fight – **2**'s intuition, because although yours is such a common-sense number, it recognizes that not every observation is born of obvious behaviour or openness. **2**'s ability to see what is in the dark – or around the corner – will be taken very seriously by you.

You know when **2** needs a change of scene, sensing – from personal experience – the moment it all becomes too much. Both **2**s and **4**s are easily capable of working and worrying themselves into a frenzy, but no one knows the signs better than you two. And, while you may not be hugely imaginative about where to take your romantic **2** to escape for a while, you are a reliable mate who has a good memory for where your **2** has been happy before. **2** and **4** are very likely (budget permitting) to have a house in the country as a retreat – and to go there frequently.

You take on a protective role with **2**, who feels very secure with you. They are drawn to your stability and honesty – qualities they truly admire. You enjoy preserving the traditions of the past, and allow **2** to indulge in nostalgia with you. Given a choice, your home may be peppered with antiques or period features, and if you live in a newer home or new city, you will somehow contrive a country, old-fashioned feel behind the modernity.

2's role, as the partner whose instincts always work overtime, is to prevent you from work overload, or from being sterile and staid to the exclusion of fun. If anyone can get you to relax it will be your **2**, and together you should achieve harmony and practicality in equal measure. You are building, potentially, a happy world to share.

Key themes

Love of home and family · Solid approach to problems, allowing resolutions to be found · Shared interests and method in your lifestyle · **2** loosens **4**'s rigidity and cautious nature · Mutual admiration

| 3 | 2 | 1 | 9 | 8 | 7 | 6 | 5 | 4 |

4 in love with a 3 ★★

This is a strange relationship – quite possibly too dull for **3** in the long run. The only way you could make this relationship even progress beyond the starting blocks is to compromise with each other on a number of crucial points. Your world views are so different – **4** wanting security and a planned rhythm and direction, **3** wanting as much spontaneity as possible in every sphere (so, just the opposite!). **4** is the epitome of tradition, **3** the very flavour of change and modernism. **3** builds castles in the air and **4** utility rooms; **3** landscapes the Hanging Gardens of Babylon, and **4** a vegetable garden. The **4** is cautious with money, and the **3** completely undisciplined. And, where the **4** likes a physical relationship to take place in a clean and properly made bed, the **3** is planning something more risky – and only as the mood takes them. One number is about preparation in life and the best-made plans, while the other is about seizing the most nebulous opening for fun.

There may be only a little friction between you, but you will feel aggrieved by what you see as **3**'s flagrant disrespect for carefully arranged appointments and plans. Why are you late? Where have you been? How much have you had to drink? Not questions guaranteed to enchant a **3**. And actually, some of these questions may be fair enough. It's clear you have differing agendas. But what is most difficult is that you may not express these differences openly, keeping them to yourself and brewing towards a showdown which seems over the top or out of proportion when it comes. **3** wonders what all the fuss is for. But you are naturally conservative and economical, where **3** is free-thinking and at least a little irresponsible. What can possibly have attracted two such people to each other?

The explanation is that opposites (and you are complete opposites!) do, of course, attract. **3** is so fascinated by your sense of system and apparent maturity, and you are captivated by the fact that anyone can be so popular and easy-going, so lucky without apparent cause, so young and unafraid. But **3**'s love of luxury and expansiveness is just the thing to make your heart beat too fast – bordering on panic. Your best qualities clash with each other.

The only possible way forward is if the **3** allows you to feel secure, and simply agrees to embellish your stable, architect-built world. **3** would have to turn their creative eye to solid, investment-conscious projects. And you would need to loosen up, listen to **3**'s imaginative ideas and refuse the urge to quash them right from the word go because they sound risky. At best, you might show each other the way to create brilliant plans and give them a real foundation – to turn dreams into reality. But both of you would have to make big concessions and act, frankly, out of character.

I have my doubts as to how this could materialize – which is a shame, because in truth you need each other to let go of the less positive aspects of your characters. You could take on such a protective role with a **3**, and **3** could feel that your reliability is a plus. **3** could come to understand, too, that you will not compete with them, or take the limelight away. You enjoy the past, so if your **3** designs a modern space with lots of antiques you may just please each other. And you love the country and **3** the water; so, again, perhaps you can find a way to blend the two? As long as your flighty **3** can get to the city quickly for some after-hours fun, of course!

Key themes

Shared pride in children (if it gets that far!) • Different values: 3 happy-go-lucky and 4 a careful planner • Creativity must be married with solid ideas if partnership is to work • 3 could unlace 4's rigidity • 3 dominates, while 4 is anchor

3	2	1	9	8	7	6	5	4

4 in love with a 4   ★★★★

This relationship rates four stars, which is more than just a matter of mathematical symmetry. Any same-number pairing carries a feeling of mutuality and familiarity, as though both people have been together a long time and know each other well. But in the case of two **4**s, there is an added implicit admiration and respect.

4s together can be lucky, each understanding what drives the other, and having an instinctive way of silently supporting the other person through difficult tests and demanding goals. You both like to achieve financial success and material comforts, and, recognizing this without apology or wasted time, there is a stronger chance that you will support each other to that end. You focus on the same ideas, and know what it takes to get to the top. Two **4**s recognize that *persistence* is the key to success, for talent on its own can be disappointing and remain unrewarded, and education alone is not enough to ensure security. Being determined is essential, and both of you share this character trait. In a love relationship, comfort and attainment aren't everything: but being secure cheats a relationship of certain stress — stress that would overwhelm many more ardent couples over time. **4** plus **4** is **8**, the number of big finance, and together two **4**s in a love tie achieve this.

One **4** is drawn to another for their honesty and simplicity. There is nothing complicated about a **4**, and what you see is largely what you get. For a couple sharing this same down-to-earth number, this is a dream come true. One **4** will respect another's mind and sense of moral honour, their feeling of familial duty and a responsibility to the wider community, too. Together, a pair of **4**s would work tirelessly for the school committee or neighbourhood, put in hours of extra work with people who need their time, and yet never neglect the essential priority of their own close family unit. All goals seem shared and crystal-clear.

What attracts you to a **4** is also their sheer physicality. Never let it be forgotten that a **4** is a physical presence – not necessarily in terms of outright conventional beauty, but certainly in stature and dignity. A **4** enters a room and makes themselves felt, quietly. This implicit command is magnetic for many people, especially for another **4**. After the initial attraction develops, an earthy sensuality is likely to consolidate your bond, and take the closeness to a different level. **4**s are less likely to have a whirlwind romance than most, less inclined to feel a flaming passion and then experience burn-out when it becomes apparent there is no real shared substance. Everything at stake in the attraction of a **4** is more serious and real, and the intimacy between two people who share this number should be appreciated.

So why doesn't it score a full five stars? Perhaps it should, but two **4**s can be a little predictable with each other, neither one extending the other into new realms of possibility. You may not incite one another to explore any individual fringe talents or levels of awareness not strictly required for a solid life but which enhance it immeasurably. And, perhaps more significantly, both of you may have a tendency to exacerbate each other's negative side. That stoicism in the face of difficulty may turn into impossible intractability – unwillingness to move an inch even in the face of reason. Two **4**s together could be tenacious beyond the point that is pragmatic or beneficial. Sometimes a **4** needs someone they love and trust to rally them out of quiet grumpiness, and another **4** is unlikely to do that.

Key themes

Shared dignity • Mutual respect • Reasonable behaviour (though not necessarily thrill-seeking!) • Mutual goals, and pride in the same achievements • Excellent parents • Good friends as well as lovers

3   2   1   9   8   7   6   5   4

4 in love with a 5   ★★

There are few areas of meeting ground between a **4** and a **5**, and it would be an extraordinary testimony to your determination if you're able to make this work! **5** buzzes and flies through a day, sometimes surprising themselves at how things manage to turn out so brilliantly, whereas you will take care to see things through sensibly. This basic style carries into a romance, and you may drive each other to distraction in your opposing ways of tackling life.

Perhaps the initial interest can be explained by 'opposites attract'. You will be mesmerized by **5**'s vitality and energy, and quick verbal ripostes. And they will be astonished by your groundedness and good sense – the way you can see through a tangled situation and make plain sailing of it. This amounts to mutual admiration. In terms of sexual tension, that, too, may come in this pairing. You seem so fascinating to **5**, with your feet on the ground and your lack of interest in transitory passions. Your very appearance of certainty is something for **5** to think about. And a **5** will make you, as a deep-thinking **4**, wonder what is at the centre of all that energy. And they are sexy – let's face it! **5** is one of the sexiest souls in the number chart. But after the initial fizz and pop has gone a little flat, what happens next? You two are just so different.

A **4** will always be trying to hold a **5** still long enough to discuss the future, but **5** is living for the moment, expressing a different philosophy. 'Why worry about what may never happen?', they think; and this is anathema for wary **4**, whose sense of personal security cannot bypass a love relationship. **5**'s flamboyance may needle you into the worst shows of anger and stubbornness; and your inflexibility in so many areas will almost certainly provoke real flashes of temper from **5**, whose patience is never one of their strong points. **5**'s wit may be lost on you over time –

though initially it has such a striking appeal; and your way of asking so many questions, and taking little on faith, is not the way a 5 likes to do things.

No doubt 5 is charming and vivid, brightening the world for a sometimes overly burdened 4. 5 may be the very splash of colour that takes away the dullness often demanded of 4. And isn't it wonderful when a calm 4 can see a way across the volcanic ground left in explosive 5's wake – keeping both of you cool together? Yet, while these truths are certain, the irritations may begin to pile up too high ...

5 speaks – and wants the world to hear – their inspirations; 4 would like a quiet place to think and get through the long list of tasks to complete before they can relax. 5 wants somewhere new and exciting to take a holiday – or, perhaps, to interrupt a boring day with a romantic lunch at the very least, or even a quick lunch hour spent in an extravagant hotel. A 4 will indulge this once or twice, but

such flights of fancy on a regular basis will seem shallow and unfulfilling in the long term: and who's to say that's wrong? If **5** wants a last-minute trip to a Greek island, **4** will panic about the rush; and if **4** wants to head for the cottage in the country, **5** will miss the action in the city. If **5**'s middle name is 'spontaneity', **4**'s is 'planning', and the two, ultimately, are on a collision course. So, this will take as much flexibility as **5** can find, and as much indulgence as **4** can muster, to work. And then, only *maybe*.

Key themes

5 loves freedom and **4** is left gasping · **4** wants to tie **5** down to fixed plans · Sexual attraction a plus, but may be short-lived · **4** is the planner, **5** the accident waiting to happen!

3 2 1 9 8 7 6 5 4

4 in love with a 6   ★★★

Even though quite dissimilar, both numbers are relatively gentle and non-aggressive – **6** especially. Consequently, any of the friction that is bound to occur is likely to be dealt with gently, and the relationship may flourish more than one might expect. Both are stubborn, it's true, but beyond a digging-in of heels occasionally, the dynamic between a **4** and **6** offers room for happiness. You are drawn to each other partly as opposites, but, unlike the contrast between, say, **4** and **3**, or **4** and **5**, this has a good chance of resolving into harmony.

Each offers the other a chance to expand their individual awareness. You understand **6**'s craving for affection and security – related somewhat to your own. No one may be better able to supply a **6** with this feeling of being beloved than you. And **6** instinctively senses when to go softly-softly every time you're under pressure. You both recognize the importance of concentrated effort to achieve a goal. **6** has such a vast supply of raw, creative talent, but not always the stamina or self-confidence to bring that to a fruitful end product. You understand this, and shore up that lack by keeping **6**'s feet firmly on the ground, their eyes on the end prize. These two energies blended offer each other a lot of support and love, and it works well.

But what drew you to each other in the beginning? Why does **6** feel a magnetic pull towards you? Partly, it's because you offer that reliable partnership they need to thrive. **6** is the number of love, and its childhood dreams and romantic ideals live or die on how cherished it feels. Without love, a **6** cannot fulfil its potential – which is considerable. Beauty and the arts, and a feeling for others, are part of **6**'s nature, but all that it has to offer is contingent on feeling that one other person cares, and that it has someone to care for. Your feet are planted strongly on

3   2   1   9   8   7   6   5   4

the ground, and this has a decided appeal.

6's essence is, perhaps, feminine in the sense of being fluid, emotive, intuitive, aesthetic; **4**'s essence is more masculine, being practical and careful, forming ideas on reason. These combine very well – though it is interesting if the **6** is the male and the **4** the female! Either way, **4** is likely to play the anchor, and **6** will entice **4** to try out philosophies and venture into fields they may never have gone into alone. **6** softens **4**'s resolute behaviour, while **4** steadies **6**'s anxieties.

4 would have to be cloth-eared and blind not to be aware of **6**'s considerable physical and sensual charms, so the attraction will be strong. **6** loves to have a partner – someone who will be on time even when the rain is pouring and the traffic impossible; and that is **4**. Home will be a focus – making a beautiful place to live in, first as a couple, and then with a family. Children will become a priority, and both numbers are proud parents.

| 4 | 5 | 6 | 7 | 8 | 9 | 1 | 2 | 3 |

6 will encourage you to loosen those purse strings and splash out for a few of life's material luxuries, and no one is more willing to work hard for such gains. Roughly put, you are the builder and **6** the decorator, and this should be a partnership that can create an atmosphere of true happiness and joy. Yes, both partners have their moody days, and refuse to budge on personal views. But there should be more than enough incentive to cope with those days, and, overall, this pairing offers an excellent chance of going the distance, if it can just negotiate the early months where adjustments need to be made.

Key themes

Mutual goals and a need for emotional security • **6** broadens **4**'s outlook, and **4** makes **6** feel secure • Good relationship for material advantages • May prefer life in a more rural environment

| 3 | 2 | 1 | 9 | 8 | 7 | 6 | 5 | 4 |

4 in love with a 7   ★★★★★

This relationship has a natural order, with 7 behaving as the serious thinker and 4 the doer, but this works extremely well. 4 is comparatively lacklustre around the noble-minded 7, but again this works to 7's advantage. So often 7 is hampered by having brilliant ideas and no method, but you are the remedy, scything through 7's more impractical side, not allowing them to be too self-indulgent. 7's worst flaw, perhaps, is to be overly aware of their own problems, and not nearly aware enough of other people's, but you'll point this out in blunt language and prevent the otherwise gifted 7 from wallowing too much – an excellent thing!

Your gritty determination to get things done and to survive hardships is just what 7 needs. A number with such a sharp intellect can be self-defeating, if it seems as though there is no point in voicing criticism or acting upon an idea just because it is likely to fall on deaf ears. Such is 7's malaise. For you, though, where there's a will there's a way, and you will put the exceptional observations and analysis of your 7 partner into a practical enough gear to make things happen. Together, you have the resolve to achieve much that is for the betterment of those around you.

Each is drawn to the other's apparent self-sufficiency and slight intellectual arrogance towards other more undisciplined numbers. You are resentful and disparaging about those who seem to make it in the world without any real intelligence or proper talent; and 7 is simply cynical about this. You bring a serious talent for practical planning and organization to the imaginative and insightful 7, and you lift each other to greater heights as a result. 7 inspires you to take your knowledge and skill to another level, while you encourage 7 to leave behind past disappointments, and make a start in the here-and-now. It's a good balance.

7 is enigmatic and interesting – which intrigues you.

3 2 1 9 8 7 6 5 4

Their plane of existence is so cerebral that they need a down-to-earth person to help them achieve. 7s are so often despairing of what the world is experiencing, while 4s find comfort where it can be found – digging in the garden, offering reliable friendship to a close group, keeping personal affairs in order. 7 needs this desperately. And 7 is so charming and funny that you can't help offering unequivocal admiration for this. Their aptitude for repartee and pithy summations will provoke you to articulate your own verbal gems – so often lost under a cloud of insecurity. Literally, 4 is enriched by 7's talents and accomplishments.

And there is a chemistry at work here. 7 is amused by your no-nonsense attitude, which accords well with their ironic take on things. 7 is often such a loner, because no one seems worth the trouble of explaining the complexities of life to; but you are a good listener, and suddenly 7 has a companion who recognizes their exceptional insight. 7 is a perfectionist, which you respect, but you understand that

| 4 | 5 | 6 | 7 | 8 | 9 | 1 | 2 | 3 |

many things can't always *be* perfect, and persuade **7** to be content sometimes with the best that can be done in the circumstances. And **7** helps you lift your attention to a more spiritual and humanitarian dimension, showing you colours you never guessed were in the spectrum.

You'll need to be forgiving of the shadows that lurk from **7**'s past: a **7** is who and what they are as a result of turning past experience into philosophical thought. That may never quite go away. But you will be excited by **7**'s superior poise and dignity – like your own, but differently expressed. This partnership is one of the best that can be.

Key themes

Common ground over social concerns • Both very intelligent • **4** the doer, **7** the architect • **4** makes **7** more sanguine, **7** lifts **4**'s thoughts up to a more philosophical and spiritual level • Enjoy time alone together

3 2 1 9 8 7 6 5 4

4 in love with an 8   ★★★

The number **8**, in relationships, if often guilty of taking too much on to itself and overriding the wishes and contributions of a partner. In fact, **8** becomes surprisingly cruel on occasion when it deems the other person plodding or uninspired. This presents complications for a bond between **4** and **8**, who would otherwise have the utmost respect for each other's code of hard work and achievement in life. This is what would make the two of you excellent companions in the boardroom, but not such a successful pair in the bedroom. **8** may be too power-hungry, even for you!

You are naturally attracted to **8** for their charisma, articulate speech and overall poise, and you both have an honesty and openness that you respect – and function with – together within the relationship. **8** fills you with hope about what may be done with a higher application of

| 4 | 5 | 6 | 7 | 8 | 9 | 1 | 2 | 3 |

the talents you share, and they are as much of a doer as you, so there is a real feeling of shared drive and the selection of mutual goals that entices both of you. But, perhaps, there is too little romance. If anything, **8** needs a companion who will make them loosen up and relax from time to time – someone who will encourage them to step back and create some inner tranquillity that can help them climb down from the destructive aspects of strain and stress all too common to **8**s. **4** is hardly the number to convince **8** to sit a dance out! Together you are more likely to lead each other to burn-out.

8 will find **4**'s concerns frankly too banal and solid to suit them for long – for **8** (male or female!) is a tremendous adventurer, something like the pirate who takes to the high seas. You hate such risk, and will want to wag a finger of admonishment when **8** takes a slide – which happens not invariably. **8** is always building up the material comforts of life, succeeding at business only to find that the wind changes, and they have to start over. This will never suit your need for security and social conformity. Plus, **8** is perhaps too showy for your taste, when it's all going well. Expensive clothes and luxuriously decorated houses mesh with **8**'s taste for quality rather than quantity – and, to a **4**, this will seem wasteful and irresponsible.

But what *does* work is when the much more expansive vision of the **8** is underscored by the attention to detail brought by **4**. **8** sees everything on the larger scale, but someone adding that ingredient of practicality and method may make this all happen. Again, though, this seems like a relationship where survival and finance can't be separated from the world of lovemaking and emotions. Business may dominate all, and there should be something beyond the achievement of physical and material things. **8** has a lovely humour, and **4** a loyal heart. Perhaps – with maturity and time – these facets may come to rescue the relationship from the tangle of material concerns.

| 4 | 5 | 6 | 7 | 8 | 9 | 1 | 2 | 3 |

This pairing rates three stars, though, precisely because of its strengths and its weaknesses. What you see will be what you get — simple as that. Neither number excites the other to those subtle characteristics of creative potential and spiritual or philosophical musings that might come in tandem with other numbers. And your caution and conservatism seems collision-bound with **8**'s progressive and sweeping manner. A possibly interesting combination, but be realistic about the romance element.

Key themes

All work and not enough play • **8** thinks on a large canvas, **4** perfects the miniature • **8** deems **4** dull at times, and **4** feels **8** is unrealistic • **8** sails the high seas, **4** ties down the sails • Functional material relationship, but business a priority

3   2   1   9   8   7   6   5   4

4 in love with a 9   ★★

This relationship demands a lot of flexibility from the **9** – which it is able to give, but will need to do so regularly. Although there are many overlapping skills and character traits, it won't be easy-going to make it work every day. If you have a developed talent for writing or creativity with your hands – which **4**s so often do – you might excite each other's creative talents well. **9** has such a way with words, and you look up to them for their fine mind and variety of knowledge and interests. If **4** can learn from **9**'s wisdom and deep thinking, and **9** from **4**'s immediate inclination to find out how or why a thing can be done, both of you might fly high. **9**, though, is not always a tremendous finisher of what it starts, because so many new options evolve, and you will find this frustrating.

Metaphorically (if not physically) tall, and having the

innate skills of a born actor, **9** enters a room and **4** is immune to the buzz. You've seen it all before, after all. But in deeper conversation, after the fuss dies down, **4** and **9** do find common ground. **9**'s insights are a revelation, and you are appreciative of someone who thinks deeply like this. Always wanting to know more, **9** seems like an encyclopedia of cultural thought. You are persuaded to reconsider long-held opinions on politics and society under the tutelage of a **9**. While you so often feel the need to keep your vision focused on the material and the present, dashing **9** suggests there may be other ways to look at life — other ideas that are important, other skills to develop. But **9** may not be so keen to be held back by your earnest questions. **9** *feels* things; **4** prefers to reason them out. And this is going to be an obstacle.

Then, too, once the physical attraction dies down (and **4** can be derailed at times by a strong, earthy physical attraction!), these numbers may not be headed in the

3 2 1 9 8 7 6 5 4

same direction. **9** desperately desires a life peppered with change and variety, while **4** is determined to batten down the hatches and prevent those winds of change from blowing through. Change is onerous for a **4**, but life's blood to a **9**. A recipe for trouble, then — at least at times.

9s can be very idealistic about love, seeking a partner who inspires their creativity and their poetic soul. A **4** will hardly do this, as being earthy and sensible is what you respect. A life built on dreams is useless for you, and **9** is an ultimate dreamer. Of course, for a while this will fascinate you, and other qualities the **9** possesses certainly do inspire your feelings. **9** is warm, has integrity, and a great power to influence other people. A **9** lover enjoys life and has a relaxed attitude about so many things, which can only be good for overworked and often insecure **4**. But if you feel criticized you will retreat into your shell, and **9** is often callous without being aware they have said anything out of place.

So what works? **9** is forgiving, which you appreciate; and you are someone with a sound sense of values and a reliable character — which **9** needs more than they would admit. Both of you like to perfect what you do, and be known for a high standard of achievement. But **9**'s moody changeability bothers you, and you may never feel secure with them. And perhaps **9** finds you too contrary and stubborn in the face of all argument. Not an easy alliance, this, but one that may give you ground for greater self-knowledge in the long run!

Key themes

4 resists 9's impulsiveness and wish to be close to so many diverse people • 9 feels tied down by 4 and unable to roam (metaphorically) • May accentuate each other's moodiness and 'self' focus

| 3 | 2 | 1 | 9 | 8 | 7 | 6 | 5 | 4 |

4 in love with an 11 ★★★★★

First, read all that is written about your relationship with a **2** (*see page 140*) – and then consider that everything that works with a **2** can be taken to an even higher level with an **11**.

You both set your mind to what you wish to do with your life, and you make it happen. Intuition runs high between you, each of you answering the other's sentence before it has been fully phrased. You are both intelligent and kind people, and the **11** will light a real fire of enthusiasm under you, beyond even the support you would normally get from **2**. And if you are a **22**, rather than a pure **4**, you have found a true soulmate. For each of you it can be said that there is no one you would rather discuss a problem or difficulty with than the other. Sometimes there may be a competitiveness, or a clash of egos, but a

4   5   6   7   8   9   1   2   3

22 and an **11** are on a higher plane, and this is worth making a few sacrifices for.

You should be able to help an **11** find some equilibrium, for this is a number which lives off quite a bit of nervous energy (unlike a **4**), and likes to work right through any project until it's realized. This can mean long hours, travel commitments, late nights. Someone in love with such a person must be tolerant of this demanding lifestyle, and here you can help. You may even prevent the overwork that is such a potential emotional stress for both **11**s and **22**s, which so often jeopardizes their ability to form personal relationships.

So, if you're prepared to get involved with one of life's achievers, an inspired light who carries a feeling of destiny, an upstanding citizen who has something to contribute to ordinary people's lives and a natural wish to improve the way things are, this may be the greatest love affair in the world for you. **11** needs someone with such a vision, someone who can break down the fanciful ideas into performable feats.

This is not to say that there won't be high and low moments, on and off days, lonely times, and that you won't have to share your interesting, but in-demand, partner with others. Nor does it promise that **11**'s feet frequently treading on clouds of light won't sometimes cause more than a wrinkle in your eyebrow, or that your stubbornness won't send **11** into an adrenaline crash. It comes down to what is important — and **11** can lift **4**'s vision upwards and out of the banal. And as a reward, life will be less routine for you, love will never be dull, emotions will always be foregrounded for each of you — which is something out of the ordinary for a **4**. You care to make an **11** happy, and an **11** cares that you care. It is potentially your best love relationship.

Key themes

4 treats 11 to a companionship that supports and calms
11's electrical energy · 11's charisma and dynamism lifts
4 to a realm of greater possibility · Both numbers live out
pre-assigned roles for each other

4 in love with a 22   ★★★★

Cut from the same cloth, **22** merely perfects the abilities and intellects of the **4**, and offers the best that **4** can be in a relationship. If you have fallen for another **4** whose birthday happens to be on the 22nd (or if *you're* the **22** yourself), you have a very powerful relationship that is worth working for. Give things time to develop. An ordinary **4** with a **22** holding their hand will find much greater confidence in their ability to take the lead in daily affairs, in business, at college. **22** has such confidence, and it is infectious.

A **22** has the power of self-belief, because everything is a joy to investigate. A **4** and a **22** together will achieve the greatest accomplishments, take their education to the highest level, push new legislation through at local government, campaign for important community reforms, and fight injustice at their children's school or in the local courts. In fact, one of you may go into law or work with legalities in some form, or perhaps become a writer exposing things that are wrong or unjust. **22** will never rest until the best result can be achieved in any quarter – and a **4** will get behind this attitude and help with all their might.

Though **4** can be an economist, **22** has quiet style – and the marriage of these approaches is beneficent. **4** chooses to spend that little bit more on those wardrobe staples, and **22** leads the way with excellent taste. The **22** will certainly take the lead in the partnership – yet never overlook the vital contribution **4** makes to the smooth running of your mutual lives. Where **4** is more shy, **22** is a front runner – but no one may be more diligent than a **4** in providing the facts that the front runner presents to the world. It is a symmetry of line and shape.

We have previously identified that **4** is the builder, but **22** is the master architect, and **4** will be happy to execute

22's plans, recognizing when a superior mind is available. This creates excellent teamwork. If **4** can be a shade dry, **22** is decidedly ironic and sharp; and if **22** can be a bit moody and down-hearted by life's harsh truths, **4** can rescue them from despair. **4** knows that the brave, brilliant **22** has a mission, and that many things under their control will affect the lives of others. This alone makes them worthy of each other's support and love.

Personally, **22** can have an enlightening effect on everyone, **4** especially. Here is a kind and honourable human being – a little too caught up in achieving the best obtainable results on any given day to notice everyone else has gone home and the sun has set. But **4** is patient with a **22**, and this relationship should have a positive influence on all those who are connected with it, as well as bringing a feeling of joy and contentment to both parties themselves. Much happiness awaits.

4 / 5 6 7 8 9 1 2 3

Key themes

Achievements will be shared and considerable • More laughter and shared goodwill than a **4** often allows • **22** inspires **4**'s self-worth

Work

YOUR **WORK** COMPATIBILITY CHART

	1	2	3	4	5
With a 1	★★★★	★★★★★	★	★★★	★★★
With a 2	★★★★★	★★★	★★★	★★★★	★
With a 3	★	★★★	★★★★	★★	★★★★★
With a 4	★★★	★★★★	★★	★★★★★	★★★
With a 5	★★★	★	★★★★★	★★★	★★
With a 6	★★	★★★★★	★★★★	★★★★	★★★★
With a 7	★★★★★	★★★	★★★	★★★★★	★★
With an 8	★★★★★	★★★★★	★★★★★	★★★	★★★★
With a 9	★★★★	★★★	★★★★★	★★	★★★
With an 11	★★	★★★★	★★★	★★★★★	★★
With a 22	★★★★★	★★	★★★	★★★	★★★★

| 4 | 5 | 6 | 7 | 8 | 9 | 1 | 2 | 3 |

6	7	8	9	11	22
★★	★★★★★	★★★★★	★★★★	★★	★★★★★
★★★★★	★★★	★★★★★	★★★	★★★★	★★
★★★★	★★★	★★★★★	★★★★★	★★★	★★★
★★★★	★★★★★	★★★	★★	★★★★★	★★★
★★★★	★★	★★★★	★★★	★★	★★★★
★★★	★	★★★★	★★★	★★★★★	★★★★
★	★★★★	★★★	★★	★★★★	★★★★★
★★★★	★★★	★★★	★★★★	★★★★★	★★★★
★★★	★★	★★★★	★★★	★★★★★	★★★★★
★★★★★	★★★★	★★★★★	★★★★★	★★★★	★★★★★
★★★★	★★★★★	★★★★	★★★★★	★★★★★	★★★

| 3 | 2 | 1 | 9 | 8 | 7 | 6 | 5 | 4 |

4 working with a 1   ★★★

A curate's egg, this working relationship is good in parts. Vibrant **1** can lead you to really utilize your powers of concentration and dedication, because they believe in you. And the incisive **1** recognizes a vital team-player when they see one – your own ego unimportant in the scheme of things, because you appreciate the importance of where **1** is taking everyone. You each have a different approach, but it's an approach that works productively.

4s have a great deal of skill in a number of areas, and **1** is perhaps one of the first people to have thanked you for that. A **1** is aware how much you add to the whole, of how your logical assessment of what is required to achieve any task is vital, if it is to move from planning-board to existence. You look at the cost, the time needed, the materials involved, and analyse this for **1**, so that they are free

| 4 | 5 | 6 | 7 | 8 | 9 | 1 | 2 | 3 |

to create and imagine new pastures. And, together, you can talk the doubters down, because if you get behind persuasive **1**, no one else can have anything to say. If **1** can make a **4** see things their way, they can make anyone!

The going gets rough when your excessive practicality gets in the way of the **1** making plans, for you have a knack for finding problems and raising objections, simply as a matter of gathering all the details. **1**'s imagination will already have taken your company to the top of its niche (worldwide!), while you're still busy working out how to pay the rent! However, **4** has faith in **1**, and – provided you don't have to live together – you should make a very productive business team. Just demand time – *always* – to mull over the ideas until you're sure.

Key themes
Well-balanced skills • Seen as 'the odd couple'

| 3 | 2 | 1 | 9 | 8 | 7 | 6 | 5 | 4 |

4 working with a 2   ★★★★

Two people who always get on well, this can be a very constructive relationship in the office. **2** appreciates the strength of **4**'s method and approach to getting the job done, while **4** has a clear understanding of what it takes to translate ideas into reality, relying on **2**'s excellent judgement and willingness to do what's required for the good of the whole. You see **2** as the specialist people-motivator they undoubtedly are; less observant numbers miss this.

4s are passionate about a job well done. Not a number to tap-dance in the moonlight without extreme provocation, you can take genuine delight in doing something difficult with precision, and **2** admires this tenacity and skill. Where you can be blunt, or forget to speak when wrapped up in a project (admit it!), **2** assuages any feelings of neglect, or fills in missing details for others. One seems

| 4 | 5 | 6 | 7 | 8 | 9 | 1 | 2 | 3 |

to take over exactly where the other leaves off. Add to this the way **2** inspires you to get the point and is then happy to take a pew beside you through thick and thin, and anyone can see why these numbers are good for each other.

There are very small dangers in a **2/4** business relationship, which mainly relate to self-deprecation and overwork, respectively. You would like to see **2** get more of the praise they richly deserve, but the mild **2** will almost never ask for it. However, rest assured you each have an ally and reliable friend who will never turn against the other. And you will need **2**'s support, because yours is not a number that sells itself to other more flamboyant members of a working group. **4** is misunderstood by many, but never by **2**.

Key themes

Complementary abilities · **2** a people person and **4** a slogger who delivers the impossible without fireworks

3 2 1 9 8 7 6 5 4

4 working with a 3 ★★

You ask **3** to settle down to duty: not something they enjoy. This is like someone telling them to act their age, and they wonder why. You want them to focus on one thing and get it done before moving on to the next — and this is nearly impossible. Indeed, **3** is at its best juggling several things at once: this keeps them fresh, and prevents them from lapsing into onerous duty and boredom. But you can't grasp this, and feel that they might be freelancing, or moonlighting, or just avoiding responsibilities. It is difficult to communicate the truth without argument, and tempers may flare.

If you could put all this aside, and accept that you have markedly different styles at the office, you offer each other all that is missing from your individual portfolios. You have all the method **3** might well envy, and **3** the social skill and verbal agility you'd love to have. You're old-fashioned,

| 4 | 5 | 6 | 7 | 8 | 9 | 1 | 2 | 3 |

while **3** likes to seek new ways to improve on worn-out techniques. This it shares with **1** and **5**, so if these numbers abound you're likely to feel outnumbered – quite literally.

But your method is essential somewhere in the organization for the smooth running of any business. You have such a practical mind, able to break down the most complicated project to make it fathomable for everyone. Without a **4**, nothing can be accounted for properly, or delegated. **3** needs **4**'s practical approach to make their ideas reach people. You will simply have to find a way to each have your own domain, because you will be driven mad by **3**'s chattering, charming, exuberant way of getting results. Chalk and cheese, perhaps – but there is room for both!

Key themes

Method versus madness · Sociability contrasted with taciturn concentration · Much tolerance needed!

3   2   1   9   8   7   6   5   4

4 working with a 4   ★★★★★

The number of high-powered, successful business is **8** — which is what you get from **4+4**. When you work with your own number, magnificent achievements are yours for the taking. Here is a team-mate who understands how to be given a work conundrum and then retire quietly to a corner to fathom the answer – just like you. Two **4**s will go in their different directions, work profoundly hard, focus to the exclusion of all else, and reappear at lunchtime with the job complete. You may even both find yourselves at the kettle or in the queue for the bathroom at the same time, because **4**s working in tandem have a synchronicity of style and purpose which amazes others. You sense each other's needs and walk carefully around them.

On any given day, one of you will take the lead over the other, only to reverse the order a week later, on a

| 4 | 5 | 6 | 7 | 8 | 9 | 1 | 2 | 3 |

different mission. You are unlikely to be competitive with one another, but highly likely to have the same level of outstanding stamina. No matter the job, you will find a system for doing it smoothly. Laughter isn't banned from your working space, just held over till the end of the day, when it can be fully enjoyed.

And if others around you decide you're a pair of aliens for your work ethic, they will admire you for the results you get, nevertheless. And after, of course, you can celebrate in a quality restaurant with excellent wine. **4**s work hard and then enjoy life afterwards – never quite collapsing into chaos or chance. It is a good pairing for business, and, as partners in your own firm, you would do wonders.

Key themes

Neat and tidy accounts • Steady progress on several fronts simultaneously • Financial success

3 2 1 9 8 7 6 5 4

4 working with a 5   ★★★

If one of you can be generous to the other's very different way of attacking things, this pairing at the office could be surprisingly good. 5 has exactly the whirlwind of ideas and energy you need to get motivated, and, once your cautious enthusiasm is added to the mix, you are the think-tank who decides whether something is ultimately achievable. Interestingly, you contribute to 5's imaginative concepts, because you ask the questions that need to be posed if a project is ever to have wings. 5 isn't bothered with such details – where the cash flow will come from, or whether there's a viable market. You are, though, and your line of enquiry will ensure that a clever idea from 5 is also *useful*.

But from here we may run into stormy weather, because 4 is like a snuffer to 5's spark. 5 functions by ignoring some of the trouble that might be ahead – very much like a **1**, rushing in where angels fear to tread. If **5** worried about teetering on the precipice, or the height from which they are going to jump, they would never perform those exciting feats that are their hallmark. **5** wants progress, and **4** consolidation – and this essential difference in the way of evaluating life is going to cause hiccups ...

Unless, of course, you can retire to opposite corners, and agree that there are horses for courses, and that each of you has a different area of excellence. **4** can find a way to bring **5**'s dream to reality, if anyone can; and **5** can cajole **4** out of grumpy resilience into change. So you can work long into the evening on a tenth cup of coffee, while **5** quaffs champagne for inspiration ... is that a problem?

Key themes

Ideologically at odds, but have complementary skills
• Requires willingness to set aside differences

| 3 | 2 | 1 | 9 | 8 | 7 | 6 | 5 | 4 |

4 working with a 6   ★★★★

Although 6 is the creative artist and 4 the accountant, you two have exactly the right blend of sense and sensuality to make a successful business team. 6 needs just such a person as you to stem their panic in a crisis, for they feel pressure personally and can be very difficult to persuade that all will be well. You represent the kind of reliable and honest figure that fills 6 with hope and restores their faith. And you are so admiring of their people skills, the fragrant and pretty work space in which they operate, that mutual respect and functionality is bound to result.

A 4 can always calm a 6's worries by finding a method that seems obvious once it has been spoken of. 6 is good at balancing the sensitivities of the rest of the workforce, blending talents and disparate feelings with all the skill of a born counsellor. You appreciate this, as it minimizes the disruptions through the office landscape. Metaphorically, you produce the solid and well-crafted 'item' for team inspection, and **6** decorates it beyond the purely functional, until something of real beauty has been born. You make an excellent team, and will be trusted by all.

Money-wise, **6** is rather lucky in attracting funds and falling on their feet, with well-timed ideas in the market-place that seem to come without much effort. **4**, though, belies that such effort is invisible – you're the person who knows how to make the money go further, and how to put the real effort in behind the initial 'luck'. So, in financial terms, this is a true marriage of luck and hard grind; and, in personal terms, you will enjoy each other as you go along.

Key themes

Smooth each other's ruffled feathers • Each recognizes what the other needs, and when • Lucky financially

| 3 | 2 | 1 | 9 | 8 | 7 | 6 | 5 | 4 |

4 working with a 7   ★★★★★

It shouldn't take much imagination to see that this has real potential. Built on mutual respect and a willingness to overlook the more intractable areas in each other's work personalities, **4** understands **7**'s need for clean, airy peace and calm and a quiet place to think, while recognizing that superior ideas are born in this superior mind. And, in return, **7** appreciates **4**'s willingness to provide exactly the right atmosphere and furnish the precise kind of data that is required to determine how to tackle a business demand. These numbers fill in around each other, without having to consult as to what is missing or required.

7 seems to have a sixth sense, as far as you're concerned, seeing (accurately) what will appeal to the most diverse group of people, and possessing the right attitude towards marketing to make a success out of a clever venture. Yet they can also be forgetful, or have a selective memory about what they have agreed or thought. Here, you rescue the missing information, and bring **7** – so often on a lofty plateau – down to earth just long enough to achieve the goal needed. And **7** comes to appreciate you for this feat. This pairing is a blend of architect and builder, the each dependent on the skills of the other, and it works.

4 will often think **7** too cerebral, and **7** may bemoan **4**'s cautiousness or lack of vision; but these perceptions will be made and stated without malice. Seeing what is – and what isn't – there, the two numbers find an excellent system for functioning at the highest level, and would make superb partners in their own business.

Key themes
4 examines the ground for an understanding of the terrain, while **7** scans the skies for signs of inspiration. Poetry!

3   2   1   9   8   7   6   5   4

4 working with an 8   ★★★

Though this pairing rates three stars, the truth will be either considerably worse than this or markedly better. If you are a solid and reliable **4**, with a penchant for accountancy skills and hours of hard work, **8** will respect you for this, though will feel obliged to take the lead in all matters of policy and public profile. But if you are more old-fashioned, and don't take chances, **8** will look on you with impatience.

8 combines **4**'s work talents and drive with **1**'s ability to see what the market will want in five years' time, and this is sometimes too much for you. Like **1** and **5**, **8** is an innovator and philosopher – and the blend of quasi-divine inspiration they receive, along with the real desire to make the world sit up and take notice, is not your favourite way of doing things. You may come to resent **8**'s arrogance, as you see it, and their wish to be too much in control.

| 4 | 5 | 6 | 7 | 8 | 9 | 1 | 2 | 3 |

What works well is that **8** will rely on your discretion, honesty and hard work to back up their lead and follow through on their ideas. You will be given true praise for the kind of resourcefulness and tenacity that perhaps only an **8** really observes. Many people take a **4**'s persistence for granted – even tease them about it. **8**, on the contrary, recognizes that, without such grind, talent is only half of a business. And you will give **8** their due, understanding that they have an enviable degree of will and personal strength that is a beacon for others. The real test will come on day one. If you can survive your first week working together, and get over the clashes of method, perhaps you are both en route to building an empire.

Key themes

Division of power important · If **8** not too high-handed and impatient, **4** is the model employee

| 3 | 2 | 1 | 9 | 8 | 7 | 6 | 5 | 4 |

4 working with a 9   ★★

Not a work relationship made in heaven, this! **9** is such a dilettante, to **4**'s mind, unable to concentrate on one thing long enough to exact a result. And, for **9**, **4** is such a stickler, always holding others up with questions that seem impossibly literal. As a number working at its best level, **9** is the conceptualist with a focus on the broader community – a universalist with an inclination to think metaphorically. This is far too abstract for sensible **4**, who wonders what planet **9** came from. Your stability and willingness to accept responsibility are a byword in your character, but **9** seems to view these traits with near-contempt. Always seeking freedom, **9** may appear to be too flaky or aspirant for **4**. Yet, there is sometimes space for success, too.

A well-educated and experienced **9** gains wisdom in a short time, learning from problems first time round. This

4   5   6   7   8   9   1   2   3

person understands how to attain the highest goals, driven by a need to complete and perfect whatever they take up. Such a **9** is able to enlist confidence from everyone around them, and you will be exactly the ally to help them. Thanks to your methodical approach to the impossible, together you may reach the wider world, and, no matter how many difficulties you encounter, it is your sense and rectitude that makes a difference. **9** can be a dreamer, but you have no time for idle wishes. If something is to be done, you'll do it, and the friendship of a **9** – once won – is there forever.

Tensions will definitely exist, and tempers may flare. It all depends on how strongly the positive traits of both numbers dominate between you.

Key themes
One works from method, the other from metaphor • Joy or despair dictated by willingness to be positive

| 3 | 2 | 1 | 9 | 8 | 7 | 6 | 5 | 4 |

4 working with an 11   ★★★★★

Just as with a **2**, you work extremely well with an **11**. The difference may be that you automatically accept an **11** taking the lead, while you willingly submit to the role of doer. You realize **11** can't exist without someone taking their genius and finding out how to make any sense of it all. You are that person. For whatever reason, you admire **11** – see it as a number picked out from the crowd. This is partly because the base number of **2** is so at home with you anyhow. **11** builds castles in the air, but you – the master builder – have the knowledge that can turn such architecture into fabulous reality. This will be truest when you are working in a creative industry together. and, if your work actually produces a created end product – be it a garden or a television show – you will leave a mark.

Sensibly, **11** knows that your contribution to the work

relationship between you is crucial and, perhaps because **11**s so often lack stability, they will depend on yours. **4**s are so often underestimated by other numbers, just because you are so engulfed in dotting 'i's and crossing 't's. But **11** understands that, while they are the visionary, you are the optometrist. Though they may be focused on the distance, you are alert to the needs of the here-and-now. While **11** is planning a project that will affect many, you are busy considering how to support the lives of the two of you right now. One is not possible without the other.

With an original and creative mind, **11** may lift **4** out of the banal, and make you see your worth in society. And you force **11** to be practical as well as idealistic. It works.

Key themes

4 provides spectacles for **11**'s way of seeing, with brilliant results • Marriage of the idealistic with the practical

| 3 | 2 | 1 | 9 | 8 | 7 | 6 | 5 | 4 |

4 working with a 22   ★★★

This should provide a partnership as productive as two **4**s together, but it rather depends on whether the pure **4** is willing to be overruled by the more far-seeing **22**. At base, **22** is a master number – and all of the '**4**' gifts are accentuated in this number. So, if **22** is allowed to have the quiet lead (and they're unlikely to become power-crazed because of it!), then true attainment is possible. **22** lifts **4**'s good sense to a superior level, appealing to their solid grasp of facts to see that things can't stay still forever. Perhaps no one else can persuade a **4** to tackle change. **4** is such a brilliant mathematical mind and, harnessed to the executive and diplomatic skills of **22**, the best things can evolve.

So why only three stars? The difficulties of this pairing show themselves with **22**'s willingness to take more risks and look further afield for business opportunities than **4**

| 4 | 5 | 6 | 7 | 8 | 9 | 1 | 2 | 3 |

likes to do. **4** prefers working with people from its business past, and is unwilling to take up an idea on faith alone. This cautiousness will probably prove well founded nine times out of ten, but there will be a decisive moment when they will miss an opportunity for real brilliance, when **22** spotted it a mile away. Frustrations thus bubble up from time to time. In a nutshell, **22** is ready to learn all a **4** can teach, but will continue beyond this point; **4** may be less generous in allowing **22** to teach them, in return.

The best advice is that the **22** be free to follow those frequent instincts that are so soundly supported by talent and knowledge. If **4** can do this – which is a lot to ask – extraordinary things may happen between you.

Key themes

22 has a PhD to **4**'s honours degree; can cause resentment
· If **4** is generous, an excellent equilibrium may ensue

3	2	1	9	8	7	6	5	4

Friendship

YOUR **FRIENDSHIP** COMPATIBILITY CHART

	1	2	3	4	5
With a 1	★★★	★★★★★	★★	★★★	★★★
With a 2	★★★★★	★★	★★★	★★★★	★
With a 3	★★	★★★	★★★★	★	★★★★
With a 4	★★★	★★★★	★	★★★★★	★★
With a 5	★★★	★	★★★★	★★	★★★
With a 6	★	★★★★	★★★★★	★★★	★★★★
With a 7	★★★★	★★★★★	★★★★	★★★★★	★
With an 8	★★★★	★★★★	★★★★★	★★	★★★★
With a 9	★★★★	★★★	★★★★	★★★★	★★★★
With an 11	★★★	★★★★★	★★	★★★★★	★★
With a 22	★★★	★★★	★★★★	★★	★★★

| 4 | 5 | 6 | 7 | 8 | 9 | 1 | 2 | 3 |

6	7	8	9	11	22
★	★★★★	★★★★	★★★★	★★★	★★★
★★★★	★★★★★	★★★★	★★★	★★★★★	★★★
★★★★★	★★★★	★★★★★	★★★★	★★	★★★★
★★★	★★★★★	★★	★★★★	★★★★★	★★
★★★★	★	★★★★	★★★★	★★	★★★
★★★★	★	★★★★	★★★★	★★★	★★★★★
★	★★★★	★★★	★★	★★★★★	★★★★★
★★★★	★★★	★★★★	★★★★	★★★★★	★★★
★★★★	★★	★★★★	★★	★★★★	★★★★
★★★	★★★★★	★★★★★	★★★★	★★★★★	★★★★
★★★★★	★★★★★	★★★	★★★★	★★★★	★★

| 3 | 2 | 1 | 9 | 8 | 7 | 6 | 5 | 4 |

Loyal and fair, with a push to see reason, you get on with most numbers – though some seem to have their head in the clouds and defy sense! Let's see which are the best combinations ... and which are the worst:

4 and 1 (★★★): **1** can be a bit pushy and tactless for you, but mostly you understand their will to get on with achieving tangible goals in life, and you admire their independence. And they rely on your sound advice and solid character in a crisis. A good friendship.

4 and 2 (★★★★): This number is a blessing for you – and you for them – in virtually every facet of life. As friends, you give each other support: **2** makes you laugh quietly at small disasters, and you encourage **2** to be more hands-on about life. Good, close friends.

4   5   6   7   8   9   1   2   3

4 and 3 (★): You will test each other's charms! You smile at **3**'s flamboyance in the office if you respect the work they do, but as friends you have very different values. **4** is rarely impressed with **3**'s instinctive way of seducing others socially, and trust may be minimal.

4 and 4 (★★★★★): Your own number is, in many ways, your best friend. You won't test each other, and can dig your heels in against one another, but you enjoy reciprocal humour, social activities, values and moral truths – and will buoy each other in times of need.

4 and 5 (★★): Hmm. Not sure about this. Rating a mere two stars, you may be better friends than this if you are at the more creative end of **4** and the **5** is physically hardy. Usually, though, **5**'s nervous energy makes you ill, and you stretch **5**'s thin patience. Very patchy.

4 and **6** (★★★): **4** makes gentle **6** feel more secure and appreciated in everything. As desert-island pals, you may be too unimaginative for **6**, but mutual interests are not the sole stuff of friendship. **6** knows where they are with you, and you love to be needed.

4 and **7** (★★★★★): You both have enough personal resourcefulness to enjoy independent activities, and your two numbers give each other credence for their gifts. **7** is more high-minded, but values your practical stance and common-sense outlook, and theirs is a number you admire. Lifelong friends.

4 and **8** (★★): This can be better than its two stars if the **8** is philosophical and can be patient. **4** can be so careful, though, and daring and courage make an **8** dynamic; a potential collision course, then. You will also need to forgive **8** their excessive largesse and inclination to dominate.

4	5	6	7	8	9	1	2	3

other aspects of your personality. You have extra charm this year, so try to use it where it is needed.

Many people find that the number **3** expresses itself in a year cycle as a third person to consider: frequently, this is the birth of a child or an addition to the family, but it might be that another party pressures you in your personal relationship. Don't talk too much about this, or show nervousness. Under a **3** vibration, it is easy to become exhausted – even through over-excitement – so be alert to the impulse towards extravagance and fragmentation. Try to enjoy the way in which you are being drawn out of yourself this year, and allow yourself time to study, write, paint. Anything you really want you can achieve now – even strange wishes and desires can be pulled towards you. Make sure you think a little about what you are asking for!

A 4 year

A year to suit you perfectly, this is a time for housekeeping, personally and literally. This year will demand practicality from you. Often a **4** brings a focus on money or accounts, on repairs around the home, or on putting your life into better order. It may not be what you want, yet it will force itself upon you. It is sometimes a year spent with a pen in hand – writing lists or cheques, doing sums and keeping diaries. It is also a year when you will need to do some research, to find out about what you don't know.

You have so much work to do in a **4**, or **22**, year – more than for a long time. Your personal pleasure takes second place to requirement, and it may seem difficult to stick to the task sometimes. Money demands that you do so, for extra expenditure is not advised in this twelve-month period. Yet, if this sounds stressful, it also gives you a feeling of satisfaction that you will achieve so much this year – a job of hard work and dedication really well done. It may be that this year gives you a very good foundation for the future and sets up lasting improvements.

You will never survive a **4** – or, especially, a **22** – year if you are not organized and implement a system of work and life. Be honest in what you do with others, but also in what you do for yourself. You cannot deceive yourself, and must check details carefully. You may have a feeling of burden at times, but there is a chance to feel you have done something extraordinary, too. Translate your clever ideas into practical results. The most significant thing for you to do is to concentrate on proper personal management. The weight of the world is on your shoulders, but you can bear it if the preparations you make are good. There is no escape from demands on your time and intelligence, but nothing can be hurried, so face the job ahead and you will soon find you have climbed a hill to new vistas.

A 5 year

After careful management of your time last year, and a feeling of being tied to the wheel, this will seem like bursting from the inside of a darkened room into bright light. Now you have a change from routine to madness, and you may feel a personal freedom that was denied you last year. Nevertheless, nothing is completely settled in a **5** year, and this uncertainty may take its toll. Try to look at this cycle as a chance to find success in newer areas, and a way to advance from necessary stagnation into running waters of energy and vitality. You will update your sense of yourself during this period, and make progress towards the life you want, following the previous year's required self-discipline.

You are admitting to the need for new pastures, so your ideas of what your life might include, or who may have a role in it, may alter now. No one likes to be held back in a **5** year, but it is still important not to be too hasty in your actions. Use your energies, by all means, but govern them with your head. This is the time for innovation, and new takes on old goals, but if you quarrel with those dear to you, or with whom you work, it may be difficult to repair later. If change is still inevitable, be as kind and constructive as possible, and make sure you aren't leaping from one difficult situation straight into another. You need to discover your versatility and personal resourcefulness to get the best out of this cycle. And, for some of the twelve months, travel or lots of movement seems inescapable.

This year is potentially some kind of turning point for you. Learning how to adapt to sudden circumstances is vital, because any plans or directives set in stone will cause you pain, and possibly come unstuck. Be prepared for changes and, if this brings a nervousness with it, try to meet the adventure head-on. If you talk yourself up and take on a front-running position, you can work wonders in a **5** year.

| 3 | 2 | 1 | 9 | 8 | 7 | 6 | 5 | 4 |

A 6 year

Love is in the air. Other things seize your time too – your home needs attention, and duties demand your energy – but, principally, this year is about emotions and relationships. Sometimes love and happiness are a reward for surviving so much in the past two years, and for unselfish service and support for others. The emphasis is on finding harmony with others, and this may come in various ways. This year, you may have the impetus and opportunity to erase problems that have previously beset you. You understand, and feel acutely sensitive towards, others, and are more radiant and beautiful than you have been for some time. If you can be kind and positive in emotional dealings, you will benefit in many ways, including materially.

There are hurdles in a **6** year in connection with obligations you feel towards others. At times you are stretched, because there are personal desires and ties you want to nurture which are countermanded by the duties you are subjected to. You may resent this, yet, if you can remain cheerful, you will be rewarded in ways not immediately apparent. Love is trying to sweep you off your feet, but your health may suffer because you are trying to fit in so much, and the intensity of your feelings is strong.

While it's good to be helpful in a **6** year, don't allow yourself to be taken advantage of, or let people drain you completely. Set up a system that lets you delegate some responsibility. Your home may bloom while you're in such a happy mood, and you should feel creative and mellow. The events of a **6** year are not as fast and furious as the previous year, but things move steadily towards a happier state of being. Let the time go as it will, because this is not a year to fight against what comes to you; get into the right philosophical gear and open yourself to pleasant surprises that come from being useful, and being warm with others.

3   2   1   9   8   7   6   5   4

A 7 year

This year is a time for manifesting your goals by visualizing them. See yourself triumphing and continuing toward your vision. Never lose sight of what you want, or confusion will reign. You'll be tempted this way and that, annoyed by gossip, and attacked by those who love you but don't understand what you are trying to do. Don't be swayed by them, or you will lose your opportunities and precious time.

Keep your head, as everything depends on your state of mind. Refuse to react to distractions, and avoid hasty actions or sudden decisions. A calm approach is the best remedy to the chaos surrounding you. You may have to move house without warning, but take it in your stride and make a calm, clear choice on where to go. If you are travelling somewhere exotic, be prepared with vitamins

| 4 | 5 | 6 | 7 | 8 | 9 | 1 | 2 | 3 |

and medicines to avoid viruses of any kind.

Legal matters may arise during this year, relating to business, investments or house options. Consult an expert to avoid pitfalls, and, when you feel happy, proceed with confidence. If you have taken all the facts and details into account, you'll now be within sight of your goal. But watch your health, as the number **7** is connected with this subject for both good and ill. You might get fit and lose some weight or, conversely, suffer with some little grievance. This is a time for mental, spiritual and physical detoxing. Also, rest: take a vacation to the country, to a quiet location where you can think in peace. Let no one confuse you. You may have to wait, but you will know how to come out on top if you listen to your intuition.

This is an excellent year for study, research, writing and reading, and clearing out all the unnecessary people or ideas from your past.

3   2   1   9   8   7   6   5   4

An 8 year

This cycle brings the possible finding of a soulmate. If you're single, you could not have a better chance of meeting that special someone than now. **8** years also relate to money, so you may be caught up with an impossible workload and regard the arrival of such a potentially strong love as poor timing – and perhaps this is why it comes to you, because your attention being taken up elsewhere may be the best reason for someone's admiration. The love vibration you experience under karmic year number **8** may point to a future relationship prospect which has a lasting importance.

For those in settled relationships, pregnancy sometimes comes with this number, and it brings a very special link between the child and their parents. Or, you may experience a deep urge to study a subject that comes easily to you, though you have never learned about it before – a

| 4 | 5 | 6 | 7 | 8 | 9 | 1 | 2 | 3 |

language, perhaps, or an artistic skill you were attracted to but never developed, but which you now pick up well. Even a professional subject that you seem to grasp quickly will seem more important to perfect than ever before. Partly, this is because **8** year cycles concern making more money, and dealing with the deeply felt past. There are huge opportunities for you in an **8** year, and you will want to be prepared to maximize them. However, you'll need to use good judgement and be efficient with your time management.

Many people feel pushed to the limit in an **8** year, because there is just so much going on. Consider, though, that the vibration of the number wants to find positive expression, so the more efficiency and determination you can bring to it, the better the chance of finishing on a high note. Don't over-commit your time or money, and be ready to acquiesce to others' ways of doing things. You need to be confident, but ready to adjust too. **8** is made up of two circles, asking 'infinity' of you. But this year, you can do it!

3   2   1   9   8   7   6   5   4

A 9 year

Your personal affairs all come to a head in a **9** year, and whatever has been insufficient, or unsatisfying, will rise to the surface and demand change now. It could be the fulfilment of many dreams, for this is the culmination of nine years' experience. Whatever is jettisoned was probably no longer of use – though this might seem dispassionate. Many friendships will drift away, but you have probably outgrown them. The strongest demand of you is a readiness to discard what will not be part of your serious future – and this can mean a temporary feeling of insecurity.

You will certainly travel in a **9** year. Even if a trip is short, or of no great distance, it will settle something in your mind. The more compassionate, tolerant and forgiving you are, the more warmth and generosity will come to you. This is not the right moment to start something completely new, but if events arise as a natural conclusion to what has gone before, this is a good thing. Your mind needs to engage with bigger issues, for selfishness or petty ideas will cause you unhappiness under this number. People will thwart you in your career and personal matters – and these obstacles seem to come out of the blue, and are beyond your control. However, if you think on philosophical issues and remain open to big ideas, everything will turn out well.

A **9** year can be populated with many friends and activities, yet can feel lonely too; this is a cycle for completion of tasks and the ending of what is not enduring. But this is the right time to see the fruits of your previous work. Be wise about where your destiny seems to want to take you. Your artistic and imaginative facilities are inspired now, and you'll begin to see new directions that you know you must investigate in the years ahead. You know what is missing in your life, or where you've failed yourself, and can now prepare for the new adventure that's about to dawn.

3   2   1   9   8   7   6   5   4

How to find your DAY NUMBER

Add the digits for the day of birth, and keep adding them until they reduce to one number:

EXAMPLES

22 April 1972	2+2 = **4**
13 October 1961	1+3 = **4**

How to find your LIFE NUMBER

Add the digits for the day, month and year of birth, and keep adding them until they reduce to one number:

EXAMPLES

22 April 1972	2+2+4+1+9+7+2 = 27 and 2+7 = **9**
13 October 1961	1+3+1+0+1+9+6+1 = 22 (a 'master' number), and 2+2 = **4**

Further reading

The Complete Book of Numerology, David A. Phillips, Hay House, 2006

The Day You Were Born: A Journey to Wholeness Through Astrology and Numerology, Linda Joyce, Citadel Press, 2003

Many Things on Numerology, Juno Jordan, De Vorss Books, 1981

Numerology, Hans Decoz and Tom Monte, Perigee Books, 2001

Numerology: The Romance in Your Name, Juno Jordan, De Vorss Books, 1977

Sacred Number, Miranda Lundy, Wooden Books, 2006

The Secret Science of Numerology: The Hidden Meaning of Numbers and Letters, Shirley Blackwell Lawrence, New Page Books, 2001

About the author

Titania Hardie is Britain's favourite 'Good Witch' and a best-selling author. Born in Sydney, Australia, Titania has a degree in English and Psychology, and also trained in parapsychology and horary astrology. With a high media profile, she regularly appears on television in the UK, US, Canada, Australia and South Africa, as well as receiving widespread newspaper and magazine coverage. Her previous titles have sold over a million copies worldwide, and include *Titania's Crystal Ball*, *Aroma Magic*, and *Hocus Pocus*. Her first novel is due to be published in summer 2007.

Acknowledgements

Many thanks to you, Nick, for the clear and brilliant vision; you knew what you wanted and, like a true and inspired **1**, kept mulling it over until a way was found. This is your baby. Also big thanks to Tessa, master number **22**, for your commitment to this magnum opus beyond call: only you and I know, Tessa, how much time and soul has gone into all of these words. To Ian, for keeping us piping along with a true **4**'s sanguine approach to such a long body of work, and to Elaine and Malcolm for the look – **6**s, naturally! For my daughter Samantha, thanks for some of your ideas which found expression in the second-to-last section: I love the latte in Soho while signing the author. Let's see! To Georgia, for work in the field on number **5**, my thanks. To all of you, my appreciation, and I wish you all LUCKY NUMBERS!

EDDISON·SADD EDITIONS

Editorial Director **Ian Jackson**	Art Director **Elaine Partington**
Managing Editor **Tessa Monina**	Mac Designer **Malcolm Smythe**
Proofreader **Nikky Twyman**	Production **Sarah Rooney**

walk out when you are cross, or refuse to take no for an answer. On consideration, though, over many days, the practical side of your **4 DAY** number may urge you to reconsider. Never go off half-cocked, therefore, or you will come to be embarrassed and confused by your own behaviour. And then again, sometimes the self-loathing you may feel about a sense of cowardice that cuts in after an initial adrenaline surge to *do* something may be acute and unhelpful. You will be annoyed with yourself for shrinking away from a fight of any kind.

At best, there is a strong chance that maturity will help you utilize the staying power of the **4** and add it to the drive of the **1**, so that after a good idea manifests in your brain you are able to find the persistence to see through what you begin. And, that overly serious side to your character which comes from the **4** will learn eventually to laugh at itself as time goes by – the **1** allowing you to see that some rules and restraints are just silly, and

3   2   1   9   8   7   6   5   4

become self-imposed limitations. Try not to let the doubts of **4** override **1**'s brilliant creative powers or imagination.

If the two numbers could help each other, much could be done. This will work out truest if your **4 DAY** number is actually a **22**, for this higher-power variant of **4** is more like **1**, and allows much more daring and a broader view of the world altogether. In fact, if you are a **22/4** and a **1**, you will be quite an act for anyone to follow! **1** initializes projects, but the **22** would help you carry them to a much higher office. Such a pair of numbers will appear in someone with their own high-power business — an actor, perhaps, or someone attracted to politics.

4 Day with 2 Life

Anyone with this combination of numbers is going to be hard-working and very well-organized mentally. You really know how to put method into any suggested direction, and **2** adds a sparkle to the otherwise dry **4** (which, on its own, can often frustrate others just a little). **2** relieves **4** on a daily basis from being too grinding and serious, for **2** is often playful and **4** needs something to help it laugh and unwind. The two numbers together, then, lend each other something good.

With a **4 DAY** number blended with artistic **2**, you are going to get through many things in your life, because **4** dislikes leaving anything in the realms of dreams, and **2** is an inspired dreamer. **4**'s challenge is to make things possible, and this, married to **2**, gives the potentially dreamy side to your character a reality check. **4** never lets a really good

3   2   1   9   8   7   6   5   4

opportunity get away from lack of drive to see it through.

Your strong inclination, from your **DAY** number, is to place your energies with your home and family, and give as much support as you can to those you love. **4** is helped by **2** here, as it brings common sense into play alongside **2**'s sensitive feelings. **4** knows when to leave a partner or family member alone to make their own decisions, where **2** occasionally pushes the loved one into a corner and offers to do too much. This is well-meaning, of course, but **4** is stoic and knows when to pull back, creating a sense of balance between the caring qualities and interfering instincts that can make **2**s suffocate those they love. And **2** stops **4** from ignoring what is going on in a loved one's heart. This is a good compromise.

With the maturity that comes with age, and fortifies the qualities of the **4** with **2**'s gentleness, material security is likely to come to you. Both numbers like to be able to afford material things, but it is **4** that brings an excellent, practical head to the planning table, and makes it clear how to achieve what you want without selling your soul. These two numbers suggest your home and garden will be an investment but also a respite from the encroaching world.

If the **4** is a **22**, blended with **2**'s sensitive soul you are on your way to serious achievement that will affect many more people than just yourself (especially if your **2** is master number **11**). You create a standard of high endeavour, and there is a knock-on effect whereby others you come into contact with feel changed or inspired to new horizons as a direct result of your example. And **22** and/or **11** are both clever numbers which benefit from having **2** as a kind of subtext, allowing your intuition to step in at the highest level and add sharpness to **4**'s sensible mind.

Politics seems such a likely place for you to exercise your skills, because **2** is the diplomat and **4** (especially **22**) works for the social good. It's a lot to live up to, but this combination will do something rather unique in life.

3 2 1 9 8 7 6 5 4

4 Day with 3 Life

You are a drama queen, even though your **4 DAY** number tries to disguise this. Although **4** adds concentration and application to zany **3**, **3** always offsets **4**'s practicality with a flair for making a life full of incidents. True, being a **4** gives you the strength to stick at tasks and to transform your work and plans into some kind of reality, but your creative imagination and enthusiasm for ideas which leave others bewildered is what earmarks you.

Your **3 LIFE** number bestows the ability to express your experience of life with gritty humour, and you encapsulate the essence of people and events with colourful phrases, but **4** makes you sit back a little, and stops you from saying inappropriate things *most* of the time. You prefer it when people come to you, and, 'Godfatheresque', you never do the apologizing. **4** undermines **3**'s normal confidence with

4   5   6   7   8   9   1   2   3

a little insecurity – not a bad thing – and your need to feel loved means that the best people always fall into your life.

Having **4** as the more dominant number, you have a more practical ability to appraise people and situations for their true worth, and your concentration level is excellent. You understand the details behind every project, and accept that work and effort are required. Happily, the **3** will always bestow humour, charm and a restless spirit, but working with **4** it establishes that vital ingredient of 'flair' alongside method, so that you construct a tangible world in your fairy-tale imagination. Other **3**s build castles in the air, but this DAY/LIFE pairing means your castles are real enough, and have central heating and luxurious bathrooms!

3 underlines **4**'s ability in many creative areas, notably being able with your hands, but you may also have fancy footwork, and be a skilful dancer or sportsperson. In business you are also capable of helping others, for **4**'s patience guides **3** – yet **3**, of course, blesses you with a more easily approachable personality. **3** extends and alters **4**'s sociability by making you more selective in your personal friendships and business associations, but much more outgoing; yet perhaps, thankfully, **4** dominates the reckless, chancy **3**, and makes you more careful with your possessions, and a better manager of your daily life. **3** and **4** working together are also likely to accentuate the more reticent side of your character, highlighting **3**'s sensitivity and disinclination for criticism. However, backed up by **4**, you are more likely to shrug off rude comments, deciding that whoever bestowed it is beneath your attention.

The combination of talents from these numbers should make you very successful in dealing with property or houses, gardens, music and the entertainment industry. You will also have a unique personal taste in jewellery and accessories. Avoid get-rich-quick schemes, but be sure **3** bathes **4** in more than your share of luck. **4** next to inventive **3** simply helps you to actualize your dreams.

4 Day with 5 Life

With these numbers, the term 'organized chaos' springs to mind! Even as the second-string number, **5** loves to paint life in brighter colours, take risks and try everything it can. This level of thrill is almost unimaginable to an ordinary **4**, but **5** has an electrifying effect, and makes much of what has been said up to now about **4**'s caution seem untrue. Although it isn't quite …

The truth is that both numbers still work at full force — **5** tearing at your soul to be freer and keep on the move, and **4** asking that you secure your life against the damage that may come from high winds blowing. But with **5** playing the part of these high winds, you may either be your own worst enemy at times, or your own best breath of fresh air. These numbers are truly at odds, and as a result you may feel tugged one way in life and then the other, not knowing why your energy and your mood seem to dip and swing so strongly.

At best, you are more strongly independent thanks to **4**, but value your freedom thanks to **5**, and you will get out in the world and enjoy life after a little good planning. **5**'s love of travel married to **4**'s inclination for research and fact-gathering makes you both a good linguist and an ideal travel-industry worker. Long hours won't bother you, and you will emit an aura of excitement and confidence that will win others over.

You are likely to be more impatient because of the **5**, and also generally more restless and energetic, with a lower boredom threshold. But you are also more adventurous, which offsets probably the worst factor of number **4** – that it prefers to sit back and observe much of life without actually taking the risk to get involved. **5** sees off such conservatism. You will still take care of the banal things of life – which is good for a **5**, who often refuses such dross and expects someone else to do it – but you are also willing to stand up for your rights and go after what you want without grumpy resignation.

These numbers are not easy bedfellows, but the **5** has a stirring effect on **4** and may help, over time, to encourage you to act on the talents you know you have, persuading you not to hide your light under a bushel. The plodding nature of **4** is plugged into a new electricity socket, and a whirlwind of activity could result!

4 Day with 6 Life

6's charm, exercised in increasing amounts as this number makes itself felt across your life, will have a wonderfully uplifting effect on the dryer character of **4**. Perhaps **4**'s most disarming failing is an ability to articulate the truth to friends without tact at times – bluntness being a **4** trademark, but not something that is always welcome at any given time. **6** ameliorates this tendency, allowing **4** to be honest and stay true to their moral compulsion for truth, yet softening this with a verbal gentleness and a feeling for the way in which necessary truths might be couched.

6 adds to **4**'s role as counsellor and good friend, helping especially in relationships, where **4**'s need for openness is sometimes at odds with the other person's ability to express what *they* are feeling. **6** lends **4** more politesse,

| 4 | 5 | 6 | 7 | 8 | 9 | 1 | 2 | 3 |

and also makes **4**'s practical and questioning nature seem far less brittle.

Actually, a **6 LIFE** number is an ideal partner for a **4 DAY**, helping to round off **4**'s considerable creative ability with more of a flourish. **6** has such a genuine eye for artistic treasures and aestheticism, and a **4** with a **6** as the partner birthday number will have more taste and take more time to create a visual balance alongside the utility of an object or space. **6** broadens **4**'s horizons, and **4** lends the sometimes fragile temperament of a **6** more solidity. Here is a person who is likely to be a talented cook, and have a practical but also *beautiful* home and garden.

The danger quantity, with these two numbers influencing you, is that your sense of duty and familial – or even social – responsibility may be taken to extremes. You could wear yourself out in the care of others. This is not practical, but some of **4**'s practicality does flee under the soft heart of **6**, which is often selfless (but not always for their own good). Try to find a balance between duty and kindness on the one hand, and self-worth and personal need on the other. You could achieve much that is real and solid but yet which speaks to the practical world with beauty and grace. These are gifts worth expressing.

4 Day with 7 Life

All of the overlap between these two numbers emerges clear as crystal, when someone has this **DAY/LIFE** combination. **7**'s nobler spirit directs **4**'s truly tireless energy to splendid effect. **7** prefers never to dirty its fine, surgical hands – but this is not a squeamishness **4** suffers from, and as a result the finely architected notions born in **7**'s imagination take real physical shape sculpted by **4**'s deft hands. And again, as with **6**, **7** operates from a more informed understanding of people's feelings, and thereby mellows **4**'s honest tongue, making it less biting or unintentionally cruel.

These two numbers agree on points of hygiene and cleanliness, so a **4/7** with a dirty hairbrush or an old or worn-out bathroom simply cannot be imagined! The bathroom may be the most important room in your house, and, along with clean bedlinen and a neatly organized office space, money spent on bedroom and bathroom would be an absolute priority. The presence of the **7** also accentuates your ability to concentrate and dwell deeply on a problem, so long nights of music and chess games, or hours spent walking in the country, will produce interesting, analytical results.

When it comes to friends, you may have only a few, but they will be loyal and true, and 'birds of a feather'. And a lover will have had to face the most stringent tests of moral character and intellectual soundness just to be with you. But lest we make you sound too worthy, **7**'s humour married to **4**'s love of the practical joke makes you superb company for the discerning mind.

And **4**'s well-publicized DIY skills could certainly be put to good use building bookshelves: these numbers put together will read their way through pretty much everything in the local library. And do you write? The combination of these two numbers gives you not only a capacity for analysis and word play, but also the self-reliance to go away quietly, sit down, and do it. You are likely to specialize in factual work.

4 Day with 8 Life

'Mogul' or 'tycoon' are words that spring to mind, when one considers the number **4** married to the superior business skills that come with **8**. This may perhaps sound overly materialistic, but fortunately there is some creative flow here as well.

While these two numbers pull against each other when seated in two individual personalities, operating within one person they lend each other utterly desirable attributes. **8** becomes more earthy, less philosophical and more in touch with other people's everyday problems, while **4** gains from **8**'s excellent judgement, impartiality, and ability to see both sides of every story. As a result, **4**'s moodiness is less pronounced, and the high-minded **8** shows worthy **4** how to be more broad-minded and less serious. **8** also raises **4**'s reason-conscious mind to more

4   5   6   7   8   9   1   2   3

spiritual questions, and often allows **4** to find some form of religious or spiritual expression — although it will always be grounded in what seems reasonable.

With its feet firmly planted on the ground, **4** is often nimble at sporty activities, but **8** adds rhythm and turns **4** into a truly gifted athlete. Similarly, **8**'s musicality governs **4**'s skill with their hands, and frequently makes a hard-working but talented soloist; you should at least have some ability in one of these directions. In fact, either of these fields may become your chosen vocational path. And then there's **8**'s insatiable desire for a fine library: this takes **4**'s literary interests to a new level and adds excellent critical judgement besides. Overall, if **4** makes **8** enviably practical, **8** lifts **4**'s gaze to a higher pinnacle. Each number improves the other's shortcomings — especially in relationship terms. **8** is a more exciting partner, but, added to **4**'s reliability, offers the loved one a lasting and growing relationship full of surprises.

The most interesting manifestation of an **8**-and-**4** combination is the capacity to achieve the high-quality material goods that you may wish for. Add to this the fact that generous **8** loosens **4**'s guard of the purse strings, and you are bound to spoil those nearest and dearest to you in the nicest restaurants or the most luxurious holiday resorts. **8** also gives you the managerial status which your **4** abilities deserve.

4 Day with 9 Life

The forgiving nature bestowed by number **9** softens **4**'s argumentative character agreeably. Where **4** can be serious and lack imagination, **9** has excellent humour and a vital idealism about life. With **9** as your second birthday number, you are always searching for greater challenges and more information about the world, **9**'s agile mind compensating for **4**'s occasional slowness in grasping new material. Where **4** will painstakingly sift through many details and form an opinion, **9** has an instant overview of the facts, and will assess a situation or a relationship largely intuitively. This is a blessing for **4**, although your sense of reason is never compromised.

And, lest **9** feel – as so often – that achievements can come easily and without effort, your **4** ethic of earning what you get prevents such presumptive habits from

3   2   1   9   8   7   6   5   4

taking root. This is excellent, because **9** has considerable talent in drama and the arts, and **4** understands very well the grind that is required to elicit something tangible from such talent. Success in such fields is much more certain from the combination of these two numbers.

9 often suffers many disappointments in life, especially concerning family during their upbringing. An anchor number like **4** lends **9** vital stoicism, and allows a greater sense of security to develop even in adversity. In other words, though as a **9** you experience and feel other's pain, as a **4** you understand how to shape a sensible attitude from this, and survive each drama. **9** is also a talented dreamer and a philanthropist, but through the number **4** you add a rational expression to such thinking and find practical ways to improve the situations that trouble you. **9** and **4** might well persuade each other into governmental or agency jobs which demand the concern for a large number of people.

| 4 | 5 | 6 | 7 | 8 | 9 | 1 | 2 | 3 |

Perhaps what is best of all, **9** gifts **4** with imagination, generosity and empathy – the very things most likely to be missed in **4**'s daily make-up. In short, these two numbers offer each other enough talent and elements of character to cover a much broader canvas over a lifetime – and with many and varied subtle colours.

THE FUTURE
Take a look what's in store...

And now we come to the calculation of your future. Each year, on your birthday, you move into a new sphere of number-influence which governs that year. The numbers progress in cycles of nine years; after nine years, the cycle starts over again, and a whole new period of your life begins afresh. The cycle can be applied to every number, so you can discover what the main issues will be for partners, friends and family, as well as for yourself, in any given year (*see calculation instructions, opposite*). Emphasis is placed on what will happen to you when you are in your own year number — that is, in any '4' year cycle.

4	5	6	7	8	9	1	2	3

Working out your cycle

To find out what year you're currently in, use the same formula employed for calculating the LIFE number, but substitute the current year for the year in which you were born. Every year, the cycle then moves on by one more number until, after a **9** year, returning to **1**, to begin the cycle again.

Calculation example 1

BIRTHDAY: 22 April 1972

TO CALCULATE THE CURRENT YEAR NUMBER: $2+2+4+\underbrace{[2+0+0+7]}_{\text{CURRENT YEAR}}$ = 17, and 1+7 = **8**

*This means that on 22 April 2007 you move into an **8** year. On 22 April the following year, this would then move into a **9** year (2+2+4+2+0+0+8 = 18, and 1+8 = **9**), and the year after that, a **1** year, and so on.*

3	2	1	9	8	7	6	5	4

Calculation example 2

BIRTHDAY: 13 October 1961

TO CALCULATE THE
CURRENT YEAR NUMBER:
$$1+3+1+0+\left[\underbrace{2+0+0+7}_{\text{CURRENT YEAR}}\right]=14, \text{ and } 1+4 = \mathbf{5}$$

*This means that on 13 October 2007 you move into a **5** year. On 13 October the following year, this would then move into a **6** year (1+3+1+0+2+0+0+8 = 15 and 1+5 = **6**), and the year after that, a **7** year, and so on.*

Many numerologists feel that the impact of a year number can be felt from the first day of that year – in other words, from 1st January. However, the usual school of thought is that the new number cycle is initiated *on your birthday itself*, and my experience tends to corroborate this. So, if your birthday is fairly late in the year – November or December, say – this means that you will have gone through most of the calendrical year before *your* new

4   5   6   7   8   9   1   2   3

number-year cycle for that year begins.

Look back over some recent years, and see if – in the descriptions on the following pages – you can pinpoint the moment when your yearly number-cycle for any given year became apparent. You'll be amazed at just how accurate this system seems to be.

3   2   1   9   8   7   6   5   4

A 1 year

This is the perfect time to set up new and quite specific long-term goals, and consider just where you want to be a few years from now. You will have new people around you from this point on, and fresh ideas about them and the interests they awaken in you. This is a completely new chapter in your life, and you should set goals for a better and more fulfilling future.

Career-wise, a **1** year often occurs at a time of new employment, or of a complete change in direction in your working life. You are probably wanting to develop new skills or make use of untested talents. You have to believe in yourself now. This is the time when it's a little easier to step back and see how to get started along a particular path. Goals, you will understand, are perfectly attainable, even if a year ago they seemed unrealistic. In a **1** year you

4   5   6   7   8   9   1   2   3

have tremendous focus and independence, and excellent determination.

The secret to your success now is in your ability to concentrate; but, emotionally, things can be quite testing. No matter how strong a love bond may be in your life, a **1** year demands that you do much for yourself. You could feel isolated or unsupported, even if someone dear is close by. This is a test of your own courage and inner strength. Only your strongest desires will gain results ... but then, your desires should be fierce during this cycle. Try not to act impulsively, as the push to do so will be powerful, but also, don't be afraid to be independent and go your own way. Strong urges are driving you – forward, for the most part – and a **1** year lends you exceptional clarity and energy.

3   2   1   9   8   7   6   5   4

A 2 year

A year which demands co-operation and partnerships at every level, **2** is a gentle year cycle, when you can consolidate what you started in the previous twelve months. You will need to be diplomatic and sensitive towards other people's feelings, but your intuition is very strong now, and you are able to share the load and the initiative more than you were allowed last year. For this reason, don't try to push things too far or too fast. After the previous whirlwind year, this is a moment to take your time and get things right.

Relationships come more into focus during a **2** year. This is especially pleasing if someone new entered your life in the last year or so, for the vibration of **2** helps a bond to strengthen, and a feeling of mutuality improves now. In some ways you may feel the desire or the need to

4   5   6   7   8   9   1   2   3

be secretive, but this is because there are unknown elements at work all on fronts. It will affect you at work and at play, and in a close tie you will discover new tenderness that will probably separate you from other friends. If there is no one special currently in your life, this may be the year to find someone: a **2** year brings a relationship much stronger than a fling!

Your negotiation skills and ability to guess what another person is feeling may work very well for you this year; and, if the number **2** derives from master number **11** (which it almost surely will), there is a chance for serious partnerships and master opportunities. You will need to look at contracts carefully, and spend time on legalities. But this is often the most exciting and unusual year out of the nine. Mysteries come to light, and your ideas flow well. Just be prepared to consider another person in every equation.

A 3 year

Time for you! This twelve-month period is concerned with developing your abilities and testing your flexibility. Your imagination is especially strong, and you may have particular opportunities to improve your wealth and make lasting friendships. You will also need to be focused, because the energy of a **3** year is fast and furious, and may make you feel dissolute. Usually, though, this is a happy year spent with some travel prospects and many creative inspirations. Difficulties which intruded in the previous two years are often resolved in this year cycle.

Business and your social life often run together in a **3** year, and work will be a lot of fun. It is worth taking time over your appearance and indulging yourself more than usual, for the sociability of this number brings you many invitations and a chance to create a new look, or to explore

4 5 6 7 8 9 1 2 3

other aspects of your personality. You have extra charm this year, so try to use it where it is needed.

Many people find that the number **3** expresses itself in a year cycle as a third person to consider: frequently, this is the birth of a child or an addition to the family, but it might be that another party pressures you in your personal relationship. Don't talk too much about this, or show nervousness. Under a **3** vibration, it is easy to become exhausted – even through over-excitement – so be alert to the impulse towards extravagance and fragmentation. Try to enjoy the way in which you are being drawn out of yourself this year, and allow yourself time to study, write, paint. Anything you really want you can achieve now – even strange wishes and desires can be pulled towards you. Make sure you think a little about what you are asking for!

A 4 year

A year to suit you perfectly, this is a time for housekeeping, personally and literally. This year will demand practicality from you. Often a **4** brings a focus on money or accounts, on repairs around the home, or on putting your life into better order. It may not be what you want, yet it will force itself upon you. It is sometimes a year spent with a pen in hand – writing lists or cheques, doing sums and keeping diaries. It is also a year when you will need to do some research, to find out about what you don't know.

You have so much work to do in a **4**, or **22**, year – more than for a long time. Your personal pleasure takes second place to requirement, and it may seem difficult to stick to the task sometimes. Money demands that you do so, for extra expenditure is not advised in this twelve-month period. Yet, if this sounds stressful, it also gives you a feeling of satisfaction that you will achieve so much this year – a job of hard work and dedication really well done. It may be that this year gives you a very good foundation for the future and sets up lasting improvements.

You will never survive a **4** – or, especially, a **22** – year if you are not organized and implement a system of work and life. Be honest in what you do with others, but also in what you do for yourself. You cannot deceive yourself, and must check details carefully. You may have a feeling of burden at times, but there is a chance to feel you have done something extraordinary, too. Translate your clever ideas into practical results. The most significant thing for you to do is to concentrate on proper personal management. The weight of the world is on your shoulders, but you can bear it if the preparations you make are good. There is no escape from demands on your time and intelligence, but nothing can be hurried, so face the job ahead and you will soon find you have climbed a hill to new vistas.

3 2 1 9 8 7 6 5 4

A 5 year

After careful management of your time last year, and a feeling of being tied to the wheel, this will seem like bursting from the inside of a darkened room into bright light. Now you have a change from routine to madness, and you may feel a personal freedom that was denied you last year. Nevertheless, nothing is completely settled in a **5** year, and this uncertainty may take its toll. Try to look at this cycle as a chance to find success in newer areas, and a way to advance from necessary stagnation into running waters of energy and vitality. You will update your sense of yourself during this period, and make progress towards the life you want, following the previous year's required self-discipline.

You are admitting to the need for new pastures, so your ideas of what your life might include, or who may have a role in it, may alter now. No one likes to be held back in a **5** year, but it is still important not to be too hasty in your actions. Use your energies, by all means, but govern them with your head. This is the time for innovation, and new takes on old goals, but if you quarrel with those dear to you, or with whom you work, it may be difficult to repair later. If change is still inevitable, be as kind and constructive as possible, and make sure you aren't leaping from one difficult situation straight into another. You need to discover your versatility and personal resourcefulness to get the best out of this cycle. And, for some of the twelve months, travel or lots of movement seems inescapable.

This year is potentially some kind of turning point for you. Learning how to adapt to sudden circumstances is vital, because any plans or directives set in stone will cause you pain, and possibly come unstuck. Be prepared for changes and, if this brings a nervousness with it, try to meet the adventure head-on. If you talk yourself up and take on a front-running position, you can work wonders in a **5** year.

A 6 year

Love is in the air. Other things seize your time too – your home needs attention, and duties demand your energy – but, principally, this year is about emotions and relationships. Sometimes love and happiness are a reward for surviving so much in the past two years, and for unselfish service and support for others. The emphasis is on finding harmony with others, and this may come in various ways. This year, you may have the impetus and opportunity to erase problems that have previously beset you. You understand, and feel acutely sensitive towards, others, and are more radiant and beautiful than you have been for some time. If you can be kind and positive in emotional dealings, you will benefit in many ways, including materially.

There are hurdles in a **6** year in connection with obligations you feel towards others. At times you are stretched,

4   5   6   7   8   9   1   2   3

because there are personal desires and ties you want to nurture which are countermanded by the duties you are subjected to. You may resent this, yet, if you can remain cheerful, you will be rewarded in ways not immediately apparent. Love is trying to sweep you off your feet, but your health may suffer because you are trying to fit in so much, and the intensity of your feelings is strong.

While it's good to be helpful in a **6** year, don't allow yourself to be taken advantage of, or let people drain you completely. Set up a system that lets you delegate some responsibility. Your home may bloom while you're in such a happy mood, and you should feel creative and mellow. The events of a **6** year are not as fast and furious as the previous year, but things move steadily towards a happier state of being. Let the time go as it will, because this is not a year to fight against what comes to you; get into the right philosophical gear and open yourself to pleasant surprises that come from being useful, and being warm with others.

3 2 1 9 8 7 6 5 4

A 7 year

This year is a time for manifesting your goals by visualizing them. See yourself triumphing and continuing toward your vision. Never lose sight of what you want, or confusion will reign. You'll be tempted this way and that, annoyed by gossip, and attacked by those who love you but don't understand what you are trying to do. Don't be swayed by them, or you will lose your opportunities and precious time.

Keep your head, as everything depends on your state of mind. Refuse to react to distractions, and avoid hasty actions or sudden decisions. A calm approach is the best remedy to the chaos surrounding you. You may have to move house without warning, but take it in your stride and make a calm, clear choice on where to go. If you are travelling somewhere exotic, be prepared with vitamins

| 4 | 5 | 6 | 7 | 8 | 9 | 1 | 2 | 3 |

and medicines to avoid viruses of any kind.

Legal matters may arise during this year, relating to business, investments or house options. Consult an expert to avoid pitfalls, and, when you feel happy, proceed with confidence. If you have taken all the facts and details into account, you'll now be within sight of your goal. But watch your health, as the number 7 is connected with this subject for both good and ill. You might get fit and lose some weight or, conversely, suffer with some little grievance. This is a time for mental, spiritual and physical detoxing. Also, rest: take a vacation to the country, to a quiet location where you can think in peace. Let no one confuse you. You may have to wait, but you will know how to come out on top if you listen to your intuition.

This is an excellent year for study, research, writing and reading, and clearing out all the unnecessary people or ideas from your past.

3   2   1   9   8   7   6   5   4

An 8 year

This cycle brings the possible finding of a soulmate. If you're single, you could not have a better chance of meeting that special someone than now. **8** years also relate to money, so you may be caught up with an impossible workload and regard the arrival of such a potentially strong love as poor timing – and perhaps this is why it comes to you, because your attention being taken up elsewhere may be the best reason for someone's admiration. The love vibration you experience under karmic year number **8** may point to a future relationship prospect which has a lasting importance.

For those in settled relationships, pregnancy sometimes comes with this number, and it brings a very special link between the child and their parents. Or, you may experience a deep urge to study a subject that comes easily to you, though you have never learned about it before – a

4   5   6   7   8   9   1   2   3

language, perhaps, or an artistic skill you were attracted to but never developed, but which you now pick up well. Even a professional subject that you seem to grasp quickly will seem more important to perfect than ever before. Partly, this is because **8** year cycles concern making more money, and dealing with the deeply felt past. There are huge opportunities for you in an **8** year, and you will want to be prepared to maximize them. However, you'll need to use good judgement and be efficient with your time management.

Many people feel pushed to the limit in an **8** year, because there is just so much going on. Consider, though, that the vibration of the number wants to find positive expression, so the more efficiency and determination you can bring to it, the better the chance of finishing on a high note. Don't over-commit your time or money, and be ready to acquiesce to others' ways of doing things. You need to be confident, but ready to adjust too. **8** is made up of two circles, asking 'infinity' of you. But this year, you can do it!

A 9 year

Your personal affairs all come to a head in a **9** year, and whatever has been insufficient, or unsatisfying, will rise to the surface and demand change now. It could be the fulfilment of many dreams, for this is the culmination of nine years' experience. Whatever is jettisoned was probably no longer of use – though this might seem dispassionate. Many friendships will drift away, but you have probably outgrown them. The strongest demand of you is a readiness to discard what will not be part of your serious future – and this can mean a temporary feeling of insecurity.

You will certainly travel in a **9** year. Even if a trip is short, or of no great distance, it will settle something in your mind. The more compassionate, tolerant and forgiving you are, the more warmth and generosity will come to you. This is not the right moment to start something com-

4   5   6   7   8   9   1   2   3

pletely new, but if events arise as a natural conclusion to what has gone before, this is a good thing. Your mind needs to engage with bigger issues, for selfishness or petty ideas will cause you unhappiness under this number. People will thwart you in your career and personal matters – and these obstacles seem to come out of the blue, and are beyond your control. However, if you think on philosophical issues and remain open to big ideas, everything will turn out well.

A **9** year can be populated with many friends and activities, yet can feel lonely too; this is a cycle for completion of tasks and the ending of what is not enduring. But this is the right time to see the fruits of your previous work. Be wise about where your destiny seems to want to take you. Your artistic and imaginative facilities are inspired now, and you'll begin to see new directions that you know you must investigate in the years ahead. You know what is missing in your life, or where you've failed yourself, and can now prepare for the new adventure that's about to dawn.

3 2 1 **9** 8 7 6 5 4

How to find your DAY NUMBER

Add the digits for the day of birth, and keep adding them until they reduce to one number:

EXAMPLES

22 April 1972   2+2 = **4**

13 October 1961   1+3 = **4**

How to find your LIFE NUMBER

Add the digits for the day, month and year of birth, and keep adding them until they reduce to one number:

EXAMPLES

22 April 1972   2+2+4+1+9+7+2 = 27
                   and 2+7 = **9**

13 October 1961   1+3+1+0+1+9+6+1 = 22 (a 'master' number),
                   and 2+2 = **4**

Further reading

The Complete Book of Numerology, David A. Phillips, Hay House, 2006

The Day You Were Born: A Journey to Wholeness Through Astrology and Numerology, Linda Joyce, Citadel Press, 2003

Many Things on Numerology, Juno Jordan, De Vorss Books, 1981

Numerology, Hans Decoz and Tom Monte, Perigee Books, 2001

Numerology: The Romance in Your Name, Juno Jordan, De Vorss Books, 1977

Sacred Number, Miranda Lundy, Wooden Books, 2006

The Secret Science of Numerology: The Hidden Meaning of Numbers and Letters, Shirley Blackwell Lawrence, New Page Books, 2001

About the author

Titania Hardie is Britain's favourite 'Good Witch' and a best-selling author. Born in Sydney, Australia, Titania has a degree in English and Psychology, and also trained in parapsychology and horary astrology. With a high media profile, she regularly appears on television in the UK, US, Canada, Australia and South Africa, as well as receiving widespread newspaper and magazine coverage. Her previous titles have sold over a million copies worldwide, and include *Titania's Crystal Ball*, *Aroma Magic*, and *Hocus Pocus*. Her first novel is due to be published in summer 2007.

Acknowledgements

Many thanks to you, Nick, for the clear and brilliant vision; you knew what you wanted and, like a true and inspired **1**, kept mulling it over until a way was found. This is your baby. Also big thanks to Tessa, master number **22**, for your commitment to this magnum opus beyond call: only you and I know, Tessa, how much time and soul has gone into all of these words. To Ian, for keeping us piping along with a true **4**'s sanguine approach to such a long body of work, and to Elaine and Malcolm for the look – **6**s, naturally! For my daughter Samantha, thanks for some of your ideas which found expression in the second-to-last section: I love the latte in Soho while signing the author. Let's see! To Georgia, for work in the field on number **5**, my thanks. To all of you, my appreciation, and I wish you all LUCKY NUMBERS!

EDDISON·SADD EDITIONS

Editorial Director Ian Jackson
Managing Editor Tessa Monina
Proofreader Nikky Twyman

Art Director Elaine Partington
Mac Designer Malcolm Smythe
Production Sarah Rooney